The
Andre Williams
Story

Written by
RANDY "Jashon" JACKSON

Printed in the United States of America

ISBN: 978-0-578-14074-2

First paperback edition

E-mail: Humblelifeent@yahoo.com

J & M Production Publishing
52 Washington Street
P.O. Box 20
Paterson, New Jersey 07501
jashon763@aol.com

Cover graphics: Toni (tirvolino@aol.com)
Pictures courtesy of: Patrick C.

Dedication

I dedicate this book to my great-grandmother, Annie. Thank you for instilling in me to have faith in God, and for always being there when I was so close to death.

To my mother, Vicky, for never giving up on me even when the doctors' were telling you I was gone. And thank you, mom, for teaching me how to snap back proudly at people who were staring at me and say to them, "What the hell y'all lookin' at?!" You knew how much it hurt me for adults and children to stare at me. And even though I was only six or seven years of age I respected you as my mother, and I felt blessed to have a mother like you.

To my grandmother, Bet it's unbelievable that you're not here so I'm writing this to you in hopes of making you proud of me. Thank you for giving me a strong mind. Your light will always shine.

To Patrick, I don't know where to start. You always pushed me to see things outside the box. You have done more than any title could bear and dealt with all of my ups and downs when anyone else would have walked away. I pray that God blesses you. You are the strongest male figure in my life and I hope you remain in my corner for life.

To Wally, my dearest friend, from G.I. Joe's to calling payphones to Nintendo to being my bodyguard. You told me, "Dre, you're going to make it and your name is going to be all over the world." Nah. Wally (Big Bra) our name is going to be all over the world. R.I.P

To the Mothers of my children, thanks for giving the wheelchair-riding-hard-headed-bossy-little-dude a chance to be a father. I have special thanks to Jasmine for allowing me to be a daddy. I love you all.

Special thanks go to Bill, for taking me to the mall on all those Saturdays. It helped me gain self-esteem.

Special thanks go to my children, I'll always be in your life, and keep you in my videos, books and music. I love you all.

Best,

Andre Williams

Author's Note

I'm looking out my bedroom window and it feels good to watch the sunset. It quickly made me think of a conversation Andre and I had earlier in the day. A lot of people in the world take things for granted. But what if you woke up one day and things weren't the same. What if your ability to: talk, sing, walk, run was suddenly gone or gradually over a period of time? Well, I'm not sure if many people could overcome such a predicament. But I know one person who could and did overcome his misfortune and his name is Andre Williams.

While working on this book, Andre and I have become very close friends over the last year and a half. If there is one thing I've learned about him is that no matter how bleak your situation is you must be solid as a rock. Andre is a man who has seen it all and done it all while being disabled and confined to a wheelchair.

Andre once told me all he wanted before he left this earth was to attend high school, have children, and get married. Well, he has accomplished two out of three. And knowing him it won't be long before we are hearing wedding bells. When I first met Andre I was selling my book downtown Paterson, New Jersey. He approached me and told me that I should write his life story. So I asked him, why? What made his story different? He replied, "Never have an 'I can't' attitude. My story is not to offend or hurt anyone in any way. It is about overcoming and living with Muscular Dystrophy."

About a month ago Andre's wheelchair was broke and it was taking a little longer than he would have liked for it to get fixed. When I went to visit him I asked him how he was holding up without the use of his chair. Andre looked me dead in my eyes and said, "Randy, the only time I feel disabled is when my wheelchair is broke." I broke out in laughter and couldn't stop. When I looked over at him he was smiling from ear to ear. It was at that time that I knew Andre Williams was full of much more than happiness. He was full of joy because happiness is temporary but joy lasts a lifetime.

–Randy "Jashon" Jackson

Chapter 1

My name is Andre Williams and I was born June 24, 1976, at Barnert Hospital in Paterson, New Jersey. I was born premature weighing only four and a half pounds. I stayed in the hospital for two weeks before being sent home. My skin was a honey-brown complexioned. The hair on my head was jet-black, long and curly. My eyes were big as an owls eyes but I was cute as a kitten. My head seem a little big but nothing out of the normal for a baby. Mothers always shape their babies heads anyway.

My mother gave birth to me at a young and tender age of thirteen. Even though she was young I still had a strong support system. I had grandparents and great-grandparents that were there to show and give me plenty of love and affection. Later on in life my great-grandfather and great-grandmother, Mr. Will McLean and Mrs. Annie McLean, the two greatest people to walk on the earth would play the most important and meaningful parts in my life.

I have only met my father maybe three or four times in my life. I'm thirty-seven now and all I want to say about him is that he has physical sight but is spiritually blind. He didn't even make an effort to know his own son. So as far as I'm concerned he displayed a lack of insight and self-awareness to my circumstances. In other words, I hope he can read this paragraph and understand his crimes of omission.

I was told by my mother that I was a normal little boy. I never even crawled, just went straight to walking. My mother and grandparents found that to be special and they thought I would be a very smart and intelligent child. Once I began walking at nine months I never stopped. I would run around the house all day. Then take a nap and wake up and start running all over again. It was like the older I got the more I would run. It was almost like God was saying, "Use your legs now because one day you won't be able to." But I was too young to understand an epiphany.

As I began to grow there was nothing strange or different about me. I was a typical little boy running around non-stop touching everything I wasn't supposed to. It seemed that I would never sit down. Growing up brings nothing but fond memories to me. My mother was very young but beautiful in every way. At thirteen she was a dark shade of perfection. She looked much other than her age. Now I don't know if my mother lied about her age or if my father didn't care but he was twenty-six and she was thirteen when I was conceived.

When I reached the age of two, everything was still as normal as could be. Being born premature was a problem that had to be carefully observed. Premature babies can

Jaylin

develop cerebral palsy or developmental problems and sometimes brain damage. But so far so good as far as the McLean family was concerned. My mother was turning into a great teenage mom and my grand and great-grandparents were still showing me unconditional love. I was living on Governor Street in Paterson, New Jersey, and life was fine.

Then one day at the age of three I started falling down. I could just be standing or walking and I would just collapse. At first everyone thought it was just a normal boy running around too much type of thing. But as time went on it would happen more and more. Sometimes I would hit the floor hard with my head making a thumping sound. Well, for some reason to everyone it was nothing serious or anything out of the norm. This went on for two years until I turned five years old. Finally, my mom took things into her own hands, and stopped listening to everyone else. Mom told my grandparents, "This has been going on much too long. Andre has been falling down for no reason for almost three years now." I still had good humor and hand and body language. Clear strong voice, and good eye contact and great judgment for a five year old boy.

So at five years old and my mother now eighteen years of age, she decided to take me to a doctor. I always wonder how my mother at such a young age handled having a son at such a young age. At eighteen, she had turned into a real sexy African-American young woman. I had begun to notice how men always steered at her walk. Let's just say my mother was gifted with very nice, big round buttocks. And the older she got the bigger it got. So most of the time when I described my mother to someone I would always say, "You know my mom Vicky with the big ass."

At the doctor he gave me a full 100% examination from head to toe. You know what I mean from blood work to x-rays the whole nine yards. The next thing that happened I don't think a mother at eighteen or twenty-eight or thirty-eight would have been prepared for. The doctor came into the room and told my mother I had Muscular Dystrophy.

"Muscular…di-what?" my mother replied.

"Muscular Dystrophy, your son has Muscular Dystrophy."

I didn't understand a damn thing that they were talking about as the doctor went on to explain my situation. At five years old I knew it was something going on because my mother began crying. Then she grabbed me and held me tighter than she ever held me before in life. All I knew was that this tall man with his white clean doctor coat was making my mother cry uncontrollably, and I wanted him to stop!

He told my mother to give him one minute and he excused himself from the room. My mother never let me go the whole time he was gone. She just kept mumbling to herself Muscular Dystrophy over and over again. Then she would look at me and start crying harder and start all over again with the mumbling. Who would have ever known that was the reason for the sudden falls? Who would have suspected it after being born premature at four pounds and growing and living like a normal little boy my age? Yes, it was devastating news devastating news that would turn my family and my life upside down. This was the beginning of a very long and painful and heartbreaking journey that I would live for the rest of my life.

Chapter 2

When the tall white doctor pushed the door back open he held a clipboard in his hand. His face appeared relaxed but concerned. "Miss Victoria Williams, may I call you Victoria?" he asked. "Yes doctor," she replied with concern.

"As I told you before," he began, "Andre has Muscular Dystrophy which is a group of inherited disorders that involve muscle weakness and loss of muscle tissue, which gets worse overtime." The doctor inhaled and continued, "The symptoms affects muscles such as the pelvis, shoulder, or face, and can affect adults but more severe forms tend to occur in early childhood. Also symptoms include:

Mental retardation

Muscles weakness that slowly gets worse

Delayed development of muscle motor skills

Difficulty using one or more muscle skills

Drooling

Eyelid dropping (Ptosis)

Frequent falls

Loss of strength in muscles

Loss of muscle size

Problem walking (delayed walking)

Muscular Dystrophy is an *incurable* disease of childhood. Muscles wasting and loss of walking led to wheelchair dependence and eventually…DEATH."

"Is there a cure for this disease?" my mother yelled.

"There is no cure, Victoria," the doctor replied. "NO CURE, NO CURE, NO CURE."

It seemed as soon as I left that doctor's office my life change drastically. I was five years old going on six. My family was on alert to this new disease I had. They were doing the best they could to understand it and accept it. I'm sure my mother and grandmother and great-grandparents cried a river. But me, I was still a little energetic five and half year old boy. I loved music and I wanted to be like Michael Jordan, well, at first I did. My number one love was rapping. To me I was going to grow up and be the best rapper in the world. I didn't care what the doctor said I had or what the statistics said. Andre Williams was going to beat this disease and show the world.

At this time I was in public school but they were concerned with me falling all the time. They had been addressing the problem for a while. I would just be walking and out of nowhere I would just fall down. They no longer wanted me to attend public school. And that's how I would begin attending Norman S. Weir School. This was a school for handicapped students such as me. Also children with learning disabilities such as ADD or ADHD went to school

Andrea

there.

ADD is "Attention Deficit Disorder" which is a biologically based condition causing a persistent pattern of difficulties resulting in one or more of the following behaviors: Inattention, Hyperactivity, and Impulsivity.

It was there that I really began to understand what *handicapped* meant. In the next year my falling was becoming more and more frequent. By the time I was eight it was evident that I would need a wheelchair real soon. The turning point was when I met Wally.

Wally was a big, rough white boy with ADD at my school. I was eight years old and he was nine years old. Now my balance wasn't too good and most of the kids knew it. Now I'm not sure if Wally knew or not. But anyway, we began arguing about something because I wasn't by any means a Goody Two-shoes myself. And Wally went for bad too. Then out of nowhere Wally pushed me, and I flew like a rag doll being hit by a locomotive. Now, I don't know why or how but I guessed by the way I flew through the air and hit the ground, he knew I was hurt and that something was wrong with my balance. Wally ran over to me and picked me up and placed me in a wheelchair. He began begging me over and over again for his apology. After my balance and equilibrium came back to normal I accepted his apology. And from that day on, Wally and I became best friends and inseparable. He wouldn't let anyone touch me or help me not even my mother. Wally and I stayed in touch from that day until his death on September 27, 2011.

Wally died. All I know was that he had fluid on his brain. Even talking about it to this day gets me emotional.

Chapter 3

Between eight years old and twelve years old I would go back and forth between walking and the wheelchair. Some days I would need my chair and some days I wouldn't. And even though I was beginning to understand my fate in life I refused to let it cripple me. This I owed to my *mother* Victoria. She would talk to me all the time about living with my condition. My mother gave me love but it was tough love. She never babied me or treated me like a handicap person. She made me believe that I could live and do whatever I wanted to wheelchair or not. Rumors were circulating that I was just a check to her. Or she could get this or she could get that with a handicap child. But now that I'm older I appreciate all the tough love she gave me. Even if it hurt me sometimes it made me who I am today.

One thing that I never knew was that the doctors had told my mother I wouldn't live past twelve years old. Imagine all that pressure on a young woman at that time. My grand and great parents all knew that the doctors had given me to twelve years old to live. They told my mother my muscles would be wasted away and I would eventually be depended on a wheelchair until I died.

With Wally deceased and my mother and grand and great

parents in my life at home, I began to slip into a state of depression. Every day was getting more and more depressing. I knew my life would soon be dependent on a wheelchair. I was still falling down and hurting myself. Something else started eating away at me, I would watch other kids run and play and I knew I couldn't and probably would never be able to. I would never be able to play baseball, football, and most of all basketball like Michael Jordan. Everywhere I looked someone was walking, either on TV or outside my window. It was really starting to get to me. But for some reason I couldn't cry at least not on the outside. I cried but I kept everything inside all the time. It was coming to the point of me contemplating *suicide*. I couldn't live my life like this. What woman would want me? I would *never* be able to have children. I would *never* be a father, and just the thought of that made me feel terrible and meaningless.

Around this time my father had told my mother he couldn't deal with having a handicap child. So he just stayed away and never became part of my life. If I ever had children I would love them unconditionally no matter what.

One day my father told my mother he was coming to pick me up. The night before he was coming, I never even slept. I was telling everyone I saw that my father was coming to get me. I felt like I would finally be complete. My father was my only missing link. I was so excited when the time finally came. He was going to take me to meet his other children who were my half brothers and sisters. I waited on the porch in my wheelchair. I couldn't wait to spend time with my father and meet my brothers and sisters for the first time. I waited and I waited and I waited till it was late in the night. My mother kept telling me to come in the house. I kept telling her, "NO! He's coming. He promised me." Mom said, "He's not coming, honey. Come on in." I still didn't believe he would lie and do that to me. I wanted to meet the family so badly I could taste it. I knew I couldn't walk well and keep my balance. I'm sure he knew that also that's why I'm in a wheelchair. My mother came out this time with fire in her eyes. I guessed she was so mad with him she took it out on me. I told her I was not coming in until he came. I guessed that was the straw that broke the camel's back. She began to beat me until I gave in and stopped fighting her and allowed her to wheel me into the house. After that day nothing matter to me anymore. I didn't care if I lived or died. Suicide was looking better and better to me but I just needed an easy way to do it. What would it matter anyway the world would just be less one handicap person. At this time all I wanted in the world was three things:

(1): Graduate from high school. (2): Get married. (3): Have children.

But even at my young age I was beginning to know that none of that was possible. Even to believe a woman could

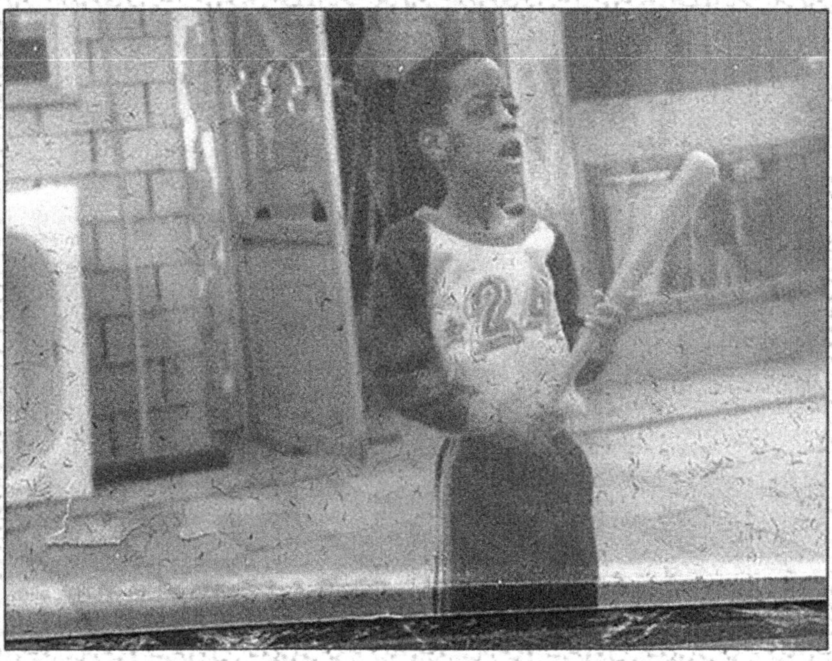

Young Andre

Life

Humble Ent.

H L E NT.

Dre

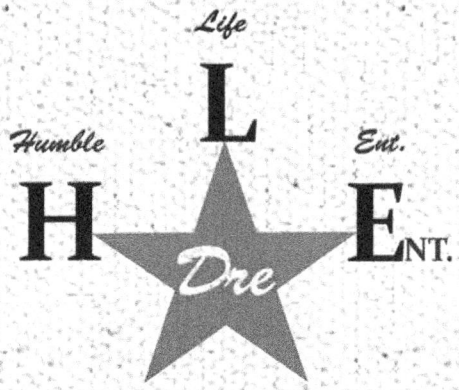

love me was too farfetched. Who would love a man in a wheelchair? Who would love me for me? Who would ever want to date me? Who would want to go to dinner with me? Who would want to go to the movies with me?

The Devil had really gotten the best of me. All day my thoughts were negative. Life seemed worthless. And no matter what anybody did it didn't make me feel any better.

Even though I still had Wally (in spirit) and my mother and my great-grandparents I was empty inside. This was too much pressure for my tiny brain. I was still very young but very mature and intelligent. I was by no means low on comprehending or sub-normal with true intelligence. My mother was street-smart and a lot of that rubbed off on me. But no matter what here I was eleven years old and barely walking and stuck in a wheelchair. Unless I found a way to end this misery—a crippled handicap and subservient life was all I had to look forward to for the rest of my life.

Chapter 4

God sent me an angel! He was tall and skinny with a brown complexion like me. God sent me an angel and his name was Will McLean, my great-grandfather. They say God might not come when you call Him but He is always on time. And on time He was in the form of my great-grandfather. He stepped in when I was at my lowest time in my life. I had no friends other than Wally when I was in school. But I needed more. I needed an everyday friend, someone to teach me things—show me things—talk to me about girls and love and things like that. Of course I had my mom, but a young boy needed a male figure around for things like that.

Will stepped right in and brightened up my life. He gave me a will to live again. He became not only my great-grandfather but my best friend. There were things I needed to know and Will explained them to me. He taught me how to work on cars. I learned things about a car engine that people in school would never know. I began to feel alive again. He made me realize that all my dreams could come true if I just stayed motivated and determined. I was in a wheelchair but I wasn't stupid. I could read and write and rap well, too.

For that whole year my great-grandfather and I were

together every day. Mr. Will McLean really kept me alive that year. My great-grandfather was a twin and my great-grandmother was a twin. I often wondered would I ever have children of my own one day. Would my dream come true? I only had three wishes and Will taught me that anything was possible. There's somebody in the world for everyone. He promised me my day would come but just be patience. Little by little I was coming to terms with my condition. I was still walking but very little at eleven years old.

One day I decided to start doing research on my illness. I thought if I was going to have to live like this I might as well find out as much as I could about it. There are many different kinds of Muscular Dystrophy, and many different symptoms to each one of them that exists. My great-grandfather let me know everything was in God's hands. Those doctors were not God and sometimes you have to be your own doctor.

If there was one special person who I could give all my thanks to, Will McLean would definitely be in the top three. He saved my life when I needed to be saved. He picked my soul up and gave it wings so I could fly mentally. That one man was my knight in shining armor. A champion without competition, my hero, and role model, till the day I died. There comes a time in every man's life when someone will come along when you're down and out and you think you can't go an inch further. When you believe that life and God has given up on you. You feel like there is no reason to carryon. When you've been hurt, beaten down mentally, sometimes you don't know which way to turn or go. And trust me please when I say, that's when God will send an angel your way. My angel was my great-grandfather Will McLean.

Well, I was approaching twelve years old and my illness was still playing a major role in my life but at least I could still walk, sometimes. I never knew how the next day would be. One day I might be in my wheelchair all day and the next day I might be walking or barley walking. I was still falling down at times when I walked. Muscular Dystrophy is a terrible disease. It weakens your muscles and your body loses all your muscle tissue. Your head can even be too heavy for your neck to hold up. And trust me that was not a good feeling to have on any given day.

One day I found out that my great-grandfather was ill. It was like a bomb went off inside my body. It couldn't be true. It just couldn't. Not the one man who had single handily brought me back to life. But that man, a man who for one whole year gave me a reason to live again and to breathe. My great-grandfather had dedicated all his time and all his knowledge and wisdom to keep me upbeat and happy. He had become more than a grandparent but a friend, a companion, my hero—the angel that God sent to me when I was in a time of despair and in need of someone.

It was all becoming so surreal. My great-grandfather was dying and my world was crashing again. But he made me strong. He made me realize the reality of life and death. Yes, there was no need to cry because he was definitely going to heaven. And one day we would meet again at the crossroads of heaven. My mother was still in my corner and every way possible. I still had love from my other grand and great-grandparents. My father was still missing in action. But I was twelve now and understanding life as it was. I guessed my father couldn't accept a handicap child, but he sure didn't have a problem sleeping with a thirteen year old girl when he was twenty-six years old.

The day of my great-grandfather's funeral was a strange day. I woke up feeling strong and magnificent. I knew that my wheelchair had become an aid but for some reason that day I was propelled to walk. And walked I did from the time we left the house to the limo and to the church. It was like Will's spirit was guiding me throughout the whole morning. When we reached the church I was still stable and comfortable on my feet. *Wow,* I thought, *God works in mysterious ways just like Will taught me.*

As I sat in the church and listened as the preacher spoke kind words after another. I began to feel a little woozy. I was sitting down and I had been feeling good all day, so I didn't understand. But this feeling wouldn't leave me. It was like I was becoming weaker by the second. It was then my turn to

23

walk up to the casket for the final viewing. I took a deep breath and pushed myself up with all the strength I had in my body. One step, two steps, three steps, and yes, I was standing there looking down at the strongest man I ever knew in my life.

Then all of a sudden I felt lightheaded and everything was swirling around. Everything started to get black. I could feel myself falling backwards. Simultaneously, I thought I heard screaming and yelling right before I blacked completely out in front of the casket.

Chapter 5

I was rushed to the hospital in an ambulance right from the funeral. Imagine that I must've of caused major chaos at my great-grandfather's funeral. I was taken to St. Joseph Hospital on Main Street in Paterson, New Jersey. As the medical staff worked on me furiously my mother was a nervous wreck. It seemed like seconds turned to minutes and the minutes turned to hours before they brought my mother the untimely sad news.

Once again here was a doctor delivering bad news to my mother about her only son. The news my mother got was not only heartbreaking but life threatening. I was in a coma and because of my Muscular Dystrophy I was having upper respiratory problems. In other words, I was barely breathing on my own.

I've always wondered how my mother dealt with all the stress from raising a handicap child without a husband. *Did I cost her to miss out on her childhood? Did she regret ever having me? Was I just one big pain in the ass? Did she really love me the way I was?*

Well, it didn't take long to find out how much love my mother had for me. Because I was told she never left my side while I was in the coma. One week went by and there was still no change in my condition. Two weeks went by and there were still no changes in my condition. During my third week in the coma the doctors made it almost clear that I would probably never wakeup again. My breathing was deteriorating every day and I was twelve with the weight of a five year old. I had tubes going in and out my body from everywhere. But my mother never lost hope and never left my bedside for one second. I was told she ate, slept, and even bathed there. I was approaching my third week in a coma when I guess I took a turn for the worst and my family was very unsure of my outcome. Doctors were called in from everywhere. Specialists and doctors with experience with my illness worked on me every day. All this time my mother was right there in the battle with me. My mother was and always will be my secret inner-strength and power. And I'll always love her for sticking with me from the cradle to the grave.

After I had been in a coma for one month it was time for God to deal me one more off the top. He would send another angel of mercy to my side to resurrect me. It was one day after I had been in a coma for a month when the miracle happened. The angel that God sent to me was my great-grandmother Annie McLean. She was 5'3" with long Indian-like hair and a true gold skin complexion with bedroom brown eyes. She made it clear that she was coming to the hospital to pray for me and pray she did. When she reached

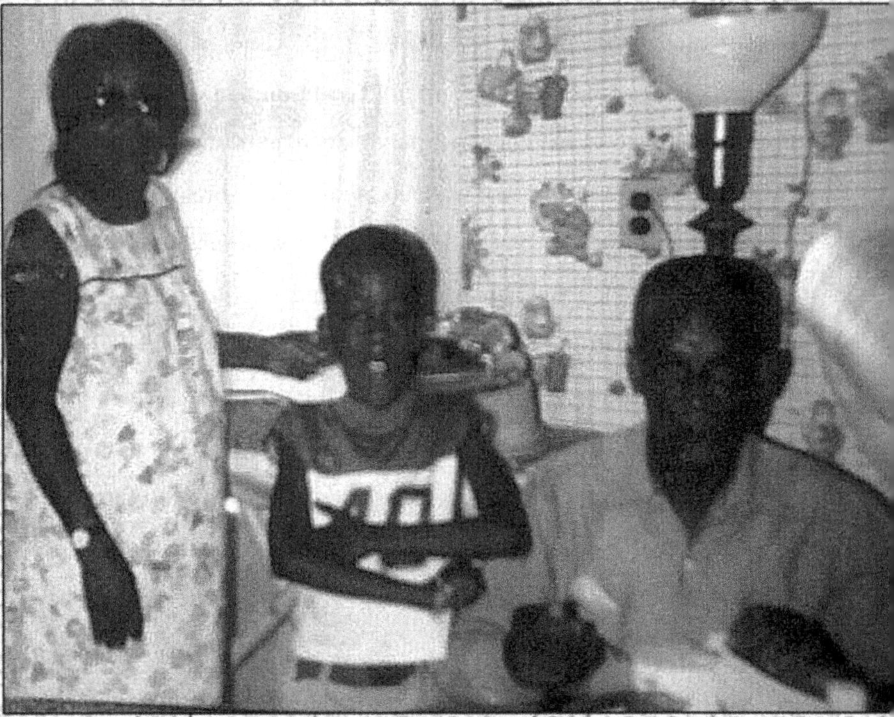

Great Grandmother, Me
and Great Grand Father (Will M.)

my hospital room it was full of doctors and nurses as usual. They were probably going through their daily routines of poking me full of needles like a pin cushion. Checking this and checking that the way they always did.

My great-grandmother ordered everyone to leave the room. My mother, the nurses, and even the doctors were told to leave the room. They must have thought this old black woman with a Bible in her hands was crazy. But either the doctors were afraid or just didn't give a damn because nothing they were doing was working. I had been in a coma for one month and one day with no signs of improvement.

When the last person left the room my great-grandmother closed the door behind them. She walked over to my bed and pulled a bottle of anointed oil out of her pocketbook. And she began to pray and shout and sprinkle me with the anointed oil over and over again. She was praying and praising God so loud you could hear her in the halls. Man, I was told my great grandmother prayed and shouted for an hour and a half over my body while sprinkling me with that anointed oil. All the nurses and guests would try and sneak a peek every chance they could get or every time they passed my room. After what seemed like an eternity great grandma walked out the room exhausted and sweating. She told my mother everything would be all right now. And then she was gone just like an angel from heaven.

That whole night my mother watched me carefully. In the

morning nothing had changed. I was still in a coma. The day seemed to pass by the same with no changes at all. Nighttime was approaching and my mother tucked me in and sat down by my bed and drifted off to sleep. I still had tubes going in and out of every part of my body. I guessed my mother was tired because she slept in that chair right next to my bed all night. When my mother woke up in the morning she tried to stretch because the chair had been nothing but pain to her back all night. And then it happened. She looked up at me and almost fainted. Then she stood up and had fallen back down. She jumped backup kissing me all over my face. It was a miracle! I was awake staring at her when she first woke up. I didn't know where I was or how I got there. But one thing I did know was that my mother was there with me and with that I knew I was safe.

It was a miracle from God when he sent my great-grandmother Annie McLean to my side to bring me back to life. And for that I'll always be grateful and humble to her for the rest of my life. Without God none of it would have been possible because He used her like a vehicle to transport spiritual healing to me to bring me back to life. I'll always love you Annie McLean to the day I die.

My mother was jubilant and eager to find out what the doctors had to say about this. No medicine or any treatments had waked me up. This was the work of God—a higher power and everyone with faith knew it. Thirty-two days and my mother never left my side. She was my inner-strength that kept me going. She told me she would talk to me every day while I was in that coma. Reminding me that she was there with me and that I wasn't there alone fighting this battle. Now, I don't remember her talking to me but I'm sure my subconscious heard everything.

Chapter 6

Now I was awoke and out of the coma but I had tubes running in and out of me everywhere. And I mean everywhere. I was by no means in good shape or out of the water should I say. I was being monitored 24/7, around the clock. My family was astonished at the turn of events that led up to me waking up out of the coma. But they also were aware of the long journey I still had ahead of me. I had a tube down my throat attached to a ventilator that was breathing for me. I had another tube running down my nose into my stomach that I was being fed with every day. And to add further damage to the situation, besides having tubes in my arms I had one inserted right into my penis to pull urine out of my bladder. All this was too much for any one person but imagine the impact it had on a twelve year old.

A couple of days after I had awoken from the coma my doctor stopped by my hospital room to take a look at me and speak with my mother. After he went through all the medical terminology and theories on what would be best for me at this time. He decided to drop more weight on my mother's back by telling her I needed a tracheostomy. Once again my mother was at a loss for words. She didn't even know what a tracheostomy was.

So the doctor went on to explain. "Miss Williams, Andre is not properly breathing on his own. I didn't think he could. The whole time he'd been in a coma the ventilator had been breathing for me. If you don't allow me to put a tracheostomy in his neck to help him breathe he probably would die." My mother was faced with this life or death situation. She asked the doctor to explain more in detail what and how it would be done and work to keep me alive.

He continued, "Well, Miss Williams, a tracheostomy care is surgery to make a hole in your neck that goes into your windpipe. Now some people need it for life and others may not. The hole is needed when your airway is blocked or for some condition that makes it hard for the patient to breathe. After the hole is made a plastic tube is placed in the hole to keep it open. A ribbon is tied around the neck to keep the tube in place. Now there are things that need to be done to ensure that the tracheostomy works and continues to work properly: (1): Keep it clean, replaced, and suctions the tube. (2): Keep the air you breathe moist. (3): Clean the hole with water and mild soap or hydrogen peroxide. (4): Change the dressing around the hole. Now the difficult part will be sticking a tube in his neck that goes down to his stomach to suction out secretion and mucus. This might need to be done 10 times a day or 100 times a day depending on the patient and mucus build up. But trust me it won't be easy or fun for you or Andre. It will seem as if he is choking when you stick

31

the tube in and he will gag and choke a little or maybe a lot, but it has to be done for him to survive. Also he will need speech therapy after the surgery because he will not be able to speak. Most of the time after a while the patient learns to speak by placing a finger over the hole and their voice can be heard. But all this comes in time with hard work and determination."

When that doctor finished talking my mother was so confused and dizzy she had to sit down before she passed out. Then the doctor told her he would give her time to make the decision and he left the room like he had just discussed the weather or what he was going to have for lunch.

The doctor and my mother not only stood right in front of me and discussed this terrifying procedure but never even took one second to asked me did I think I could breathe on my own. I was scared to death but the most irritating thing was that I believed I could breathe on my own. I just had no way of telling my mother or the doctor with a tube down my throat. I tried everything: eye movement, finger gestures, and even facial frowns but to no avail nobody knew what I was trying to say. After a while I gave up. It looked like I was headed for that cold table and that cold room to have a hole cut in my throat. Bad enough I was going to be in a wheelchair but also with a hole in my throat and not being able to talk for God knows how long. After talking it over with my grand and great-grandparents it was official like a referee with a whistle. Damn. I could have really used my father there maybe he would have held out and kept it from being a unanimous decision. Even though I never got to cast my vote; because it would have definitely been thumps down. No holes in my throat I'm going to breathe on my own. I told myself, watch and see. But my vote fell on death ears because it was never considered or asked or even contemplated.

Chapter 7

I woke up in the recovery room. If you ever had a sore throat multiple that times 1000. My throat was on fire. I was trying to cry but I couldn't. I was trying to talk but I couldn't do that either. "Andre, Andre, you're in the recovery room, okay." It seemed like the nurse kept saying the same thing over and over again. "Are you okay?" "Are you in pain?" "You're in the recovery room, Andre," she said. *Am I in pain, are you insane lady. They just cut a hole in my windpipe. I'm in more than pain I'm delirious*, I said in my mind. "Your mother is on her way in here now, Andre," she said. That was the best thing I heard since that nurse first started talking. *Get me my mommy, please!*

After motherly love and affection and about 10 or 20 cc of morphine or something I began to feel better. I'm not really sure if it was morphine but let's just say that for now. Because whatever it was it had me feeling quite nice and flying. Trust me I was only twelve but I was by no means naïve to what medicine could and would do if given the right stuff. All and all regardless to what, they could have given me nitro glycerin if that would have taken the pain away I was cool with that.

Trust me from that moment on my life would again

34

change drastically. I would never walk again. I was completely depended on my mother and great-grandmother. And to top it off I couldn't even say one word. My home had to be handicap accessible. Most of the time I stayed at my great-grandmother's house, but I would bounce back in forth from my mother house to my great-grandmother house. My great-grandmother lived in a senior citizen building and my mother lived almost next door, you could say, because the only thing that separated their houses was a long fence.

So on went my life now with a tracheostomy and a wheelchair. Trust me my mother was like a solider with my tracheostomy care. She was right on time with the changes and right on time with the suctions. Let me say one thing before I forget, nowadays it's much easier than when I was a kid. The medical field has done a great job of making the tracheostomy care a whole lot easier and better. I remember those days trying to get use to my mother having to suction the secretion out of my stomach. Just imagine the feeling of someone sticking a long object down your throat. Trust me it's nothing to write home about. Now we're talking about anywhere from 10 to 50 times a day. And even though I still have to suction the mucus some days more than others, you have to remember I was only a teenager back then. Having a tracheostomy was the last thing on my mind. I was beginning to see and want more. I was beginning to understand my situation. And knowing I had to live like this

35

Ray Jr. (son)

for the rest of my life. Also, remember my mother never treated me like a handicap she gave me very tough love. She was preparing me for the world and the many hardships I would endure in my life. And that's why I'll always love my mom. She was my inner-strength and my great teacher of life.

Knowing that I would never see my great-grandfather again was a pain that I kept hidden deep inside my soul. He was my friend and companion when I had no kid friends my age. He meant so much to me and to wake up and realize that I had passed out at his casket was a picture I couldn't get out of my mind.

This was a pain that I carried around with me for years or should I say still carry. I often wondered why on my great-grandfather's funeral day I collapsed. On the other hand, why that was the last day God permitted me to walk. Could it have been some supernatural higher power thing going on between God, myself, and my great-grandfather? Was my great-grandfather an angel? He gave me inspiration when I had none. He gave me a reason to live and fight on when life seemed so meaningless. My life had floated so far away and he brought it back and gave me purpose. There were so many things I learned from my great-grandfather that I could go on for days.

I was now really beginning to understand my life. I didn't know why I was born with muscular dystrophy, but I was a teenager now and wanted to know more about it. I knew I would have to educate myself a lot more. I started reading about conditions and affect all the time. I would read about the diagnosis, etiology, pathology and impairments of body functions and structures.

And what I learned was Duchenne Muscular Dystrophy is the most common muscular dystrophy and is a fatal disease causing progressive weakness of the skeletal and respiratory muscles. Boys with DMD are generally clumsy, may walk on their toes, and show gross motor regression over time. One thing I knew was that it was fatal in adolescence or early childhood. It also caused motor skills regression and loss of ambulation.

After I read so much about the dangers I began to question my purpose in life. One thing for sure I knew I still had my mother, great and grandparents except for my great-grandfather. Also, I knew I was still alive no matter what I had been through. I was still alive.

Andre Williams was still *alive*!

Chapter 8

For the next four years I never uttered a word. I still couldn't talk since the tracheostomy had been placed in my windpipe. I was seventeen now going on eighteen and my head was too heavy for my body. I still was in the wheelchair and 100 percent depended on care from my mother. My mother would sit me outside in front of the house in my chair all the time. The whole world was moving except for me. All I could do was sit there with my head leaned to one side and watch people and life pass me by. Some kids would just stare at me as if I was a monster. Kids can be so evil sometimes to people with disabilities. Grownups can show their ignorant side too. But all and all my mother held her head up and made me feel and believe that I was somewhat normal.

There was another small thing that started to bother me. Maybe I should say a big thing; I began to notice girls and their beauty. It began to eat at me a little at a time until it was overwhelming. But what was I going to do with a girl and what girl would even take time to acknowledge me. I couldn't walk or talk or even hold my own head up straight. And to top it all off I had a hole in my throat.

One day while my mother was cooking I started trying to

talk. I was lying down in the bed and began trying to utter out a word or a sound or anything. It wasn't the first time I had been trying to speak for more than a year or two. But for some strange reason this time I put my finger over the hole in my tracheostomy. Then I tried to say, "Mom." At first it came out like a goggling sound, "Mommmm, Mommmm," Mommmm." My mother spun around and looked to see where the sounds were coming from. When she noticed it was me, she ran over to the bed and said, "Andre, you're talking!" I just kept saying, "Mommmm" over and over again. One, it felt good to hear my voice again. And two, I was afraid to stop because I didn't know if I would be able to keep talking. My mother just fell to her knees and began crying and thanking God. I often wondered what a sight we must have been in that room with me saying, "Mommmm" over and over again, and my mother crying and screaming and praising God. That must have gone on for an hour and I mean an hour.

It had been four long years since I had uttered my last word on the day my great-grandfather's funeral was held. And believe me it seemed like a lifetime to me. Here it was again, another miracle when after about two years it was assumed that I would never talk again. From that day on I never shut up. Well, maybe when I was sleeping but that's it. Finally something good had happened to me when I had nothing else going in my favor. To be able to *talk, talk* to people like my family, and maybe even friends, and most important out of all, to be able to talk to girls even just to say "hello" or "how are you" or "have a nice day" was something beyond amazing.

Anyway, it was wonderful to be able to talk again.

Sometime after, my mother enrolled me in a great school in Clifton, New Jersey, for handicapped kids. Now that I could talk it was easier for me to attend school because I could communicate with others. I wasn't sure how it would turnout but I was eager to go, to be around other kids my age and talk to them and have friends.

Now I had friends and was able to talk to everyone my teachers and even females. But I don't know something was still missing from my life. I didn't know how people would accept seeing two handicap people, a male and a female at the movies or out for ice cream. I guess my teenage hormones and my mind was running wild. I was still a boy regardless of what. And all teenagers want boyfriends and girlfriends. Well, I guess I wanted a girlfriend too.

In school I would talk to other girls in wheelchairs like myself. And after a while we would even do a little experimental touching with each other. But that's not what I wanted out of a girl; I wanted to talk to them on the phone. I wanted to go to the mall and visit the game rooms. Maybe even go on a lunch date or to the movies.

Even though school was fun and I was learning every day

My Mom

and had friends it wasn't enough. When you're handicapped you always find yourself wondering: why me and what you can do. I was finally accomplishing one of my three things I wanted to do in my life. I was in high school and I was proud of that. But like I said before there were three things I always wanted to do in my life before I died: (1): Graduate from high school. (2): Get married. (3): Have children.

I was in high school so I guess one out of three wasn't that bad. With everything I had been through one out of three was great! I knew no one would ever want to have kids with me, let alone marry me. I mean, look at me. I have a hole in my windpipe. I'm in a wheelchair. And my head is too heavy for my own body. And I'm depended on family to care for me. I could never live alone in my own apartment and raise a family anyway.

I was stuck in my own little world and couldn't find my way out. But there was one bright spot. There was a teacher at my school who took me under his wing. I really wished I could remember his name but I can't. He was a tall white man with the biggest smile in the universe. He was very masculine and clean-cut. I'll never know what he saw in me but just like my past experiences in life, just when I thought I couldn't go on or would just give up an angel would appear. This time it was in the form of one of my high school teachers. He met my family and immediately they fell for him. This teacher made coming to school every day worthwhile. He would always manage to keep a smile on my face. Let me share one thing with you readers out there in the world. Now I don't know much about racist people or racism in the world. I was born with a disability and some people can be so evil that evil becomes as real as death. But this man, this white man, who became more than just a teacher, more than just a friend, taught me that there is good in everybody.

Here I was an African-American teenager from Paterson, New Jersey, with no father. Born with Muscular Dystrophy and given *twelve* years to live. In a coma for one month only to wake up and have a hole cut in my neck and a tracheostomy placed in my windpipe. Then to go four years without even speaking one word out my mouth, then have this gentle kind man become attached to me made me feel heavenly. He played a giant part in my life and even though I can't remember his name I'm sure he has been blessed a thousand times over for coming into my life and giving me strength, purpose, and hope to carryon.

Chapter 9

One day while I was sitting outside in my wheelchair I saw this young Hispanic-looking guy come out my building. I had been seeing a lot of him in the last couple of weeks. He had slick-looking curly hair that had a certain wave to it. He looked about fourteen or fifteen years old. His complexion was honey-brown. He was short but you could see his character and disposition was tall. This guy had the pretty boy look from head to toe and he knew it. The amazing thing about him was every time he saw me outside sitting in my wheelchair he would go out his way to speak to me and hold brief conversations.

As time went on I found out that he lived upstairs from me. His name was Angel. And he was mixed with Spanish and African-American. Every time he saw me outside in that wheelchair he would stop and talk to me longer and longer. Before long, Angel became my second real friend. Wally was my first back in elementary school. But this was different. This was my first friend outside of school who would build a bond with me. Before long we were together every day. My family loved him and his family loved me.

Angel started taking me places with him every day. He was street-smart and was very popular around the

43

neighborhood. At that time I didn't have a powered wheelchair so everywhere we went he had to push me. He would take me with him to hang out with him and his other friends. There I was wheelchair and all right on the corner with Angel and all his boys. Immediately they all took a liking to me. Angel was well-respected wherever he went, so I became respected too. I can't even start to explain how I felt with real friends who really liked me. Angel would push me everywhere and all over Paterson. But most of the time we all just hung out on the corner shooting the breeze and having a good time. Well, really if you know Paterson, you know it was a little bit more than shooting the breeze going on. Some of the guys were involved in illegal activities. I didn't care what they were doing as long as they accepted me it was cool with me.

Before long I was no longer just Andre, everybody was calling me "Dre." That was my street name and it made me feel cool and down. I even told my mom to start calling me "Dre" instead of Andre. The friendship Angel and I had been unbreakable. Angel watched over me and always had my back. Girls would come by and I would watch all the guys talking slick to them. Angel was a girl magnet with his movie star looks. They would speak to me but I knew that's as far as it would ever go. Sometimes I felt depressed that I couldn't walk and talk likes a normal kid. Many days and nights I wondered would there ever be a girl for me. I longed for a girlfriend like the other guys my age.

So I starting quizzing my mother on certain things I saw while up on the corner with Angel. She told me anything I wanted to know or do to make sure I let her know first. My mom was cool like that and still is to this day. I often saw the guys on the corner smoking marijuana. Angel smoked marijuana too with his boys on the corner. I wanted to try it but I was afraid with my condition and all. I mean, hey, I had a hole in my neck remember. But hole in neck in all I wanted to try marijuana. I knew my mother smoked it and maybe did other things too. I had begun to notice slight changes in my mom mood at times. You know like you can tell the difference between someone that's high on marijuana or drunk off liquor.

But hanging with Angel and the crew made me wise to a lot more than marijuana and liquor. They educated me on all drugs from marijuana to cocaine. At that time crack cocaine was very popular and taking over the city. Lord knows I prayed a million times my mother wasn't smoking crack cocaine.

Well, anyway, one day I got up enough nerve to ask my mother could I try marijuana? And to my amazement she said yes, as long as it was with her and in the house. So she went in her room and after about five minutes she returned with the marijuana rolled up. She explained to me how to smoke it even though I already knew from watching the guys

45

on the corner. But I listened and pretended that she had my full attention. When she gave it to me I put it in my mouth and took a short quick pull. Then I took a longer pull and held the smoke in deep down in my lungs. I started coughing as I exhaled the smoke from my lungs. My mother asked me was I alright? I nodded my head in a yes gesture. She was watching me like I was about to jump out my chair and start talking in tongues or something. I guess she was just making sure I didn't have a bad reaction to the drug.

At first I felt nothing at all. Then all of a sudden I felt light. It seemed like I was looking at things but from a tilted view. All of a sudden it was like I was floating up out of my chair but looking down at myself in the chair. I began to laugh and giggle for no apparent reason at all. My mother passed the joint back to me and I took three more deep pulls. But it still seemed like I was floating in air watching my mother and myself in my wheelchair smoking. I felt a certain surge of power and strength. I felt heavenly and light as a feather. My mind was racing a 100 miles per hour. I couldn't keep my mind on one thought for too long. I was having one beautiful thought after another. All of a sudden I had a urge to talk to a female, any female. I would sure have some slick words for her now. I would make her understand and see beyond this hole in my throat and this stupid chair. My mother and I talked for hours after that. My mother was one cool lady and she made me understand life as it really is.

Now I know to a lot of people she was a hundred percent dead wrong for smoking marijuana with me that day. But let me say one thing if she had denied me I would have done it anyway with Angel and the boys. My mom always wanted us to have no secrets between us. And anything I wanted to know to make sure I went to her first before I did it somewhere else and got in trouble or more important lost my life. After that day I was smoking every chance I got. If it wasn't with Angel it was with my mom. My urge to talk to girls was also growing larger every day. And the marijuana only intensified my urge and need to talk to girls like other boys did.

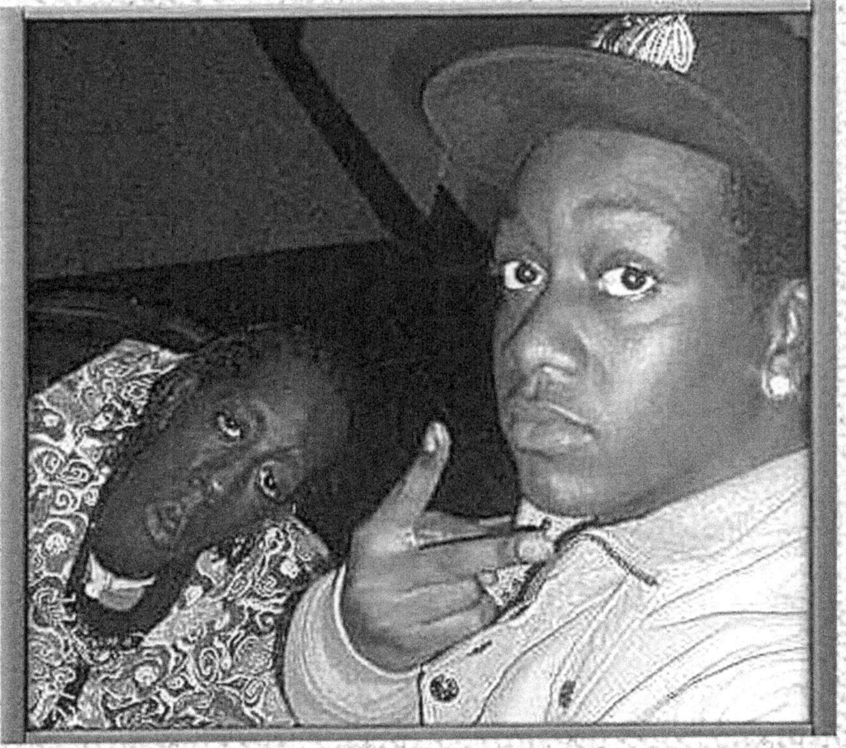

Andre & Cousin Shabba

Life

Humble Ent.

H L E NT.

Dre

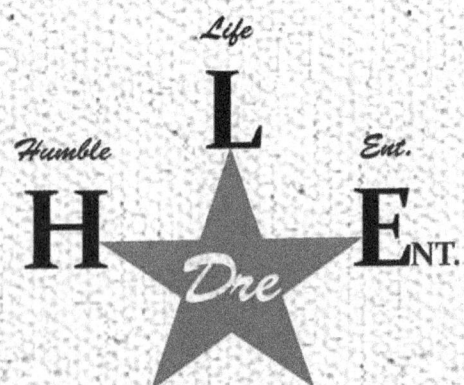

Chapter 10

One day, my teacher from high school asked me did I want to go to the mall. Bill was his name, I just remembered. Well, anyway, Bill asked me did I want to go to the mall. Of course I wanted to go to the mall. But I didn't want to go there alone. With Bill it would have been alright but I wanted to bring Angel with me. So I told him and he agreed. So Bill would come to Paterson and pick me up with my wheelchair and also Angel. He would drop us off at the Garden State Plaza mall and give us money to play games and go to the movies. Of course it was all with my mother's permission. Then he would tell us what time to meet him when he arrived to pick us up. Now what would make this man, this white man from Clifton, New Jersey, do all this out the kindness of his heart? I'll never know.

Angel and I would have the time of our lives at the mall. We would play arcade games for hours. Then sometimes we would go check out a movie. I felt alive at the mall around other kids. It didn't matter that I was in a wheelchair I was out in the world just me and my partner. Going to the mall became an every weekend event for us. Bill never missed a weekend showing up to take me and Angel to the mall. We never needed a dime; Bill would give us money every time we went there. Angel was a true friend to me. He never looked at me like I was a handicapped kid. He treated me like I was his blood brother.

There would be hundreds of girls at the mall. Angel had no problem talking to girls or getting their phone numbers. I would just watch him and smile at his slickness. Girls would speak to me and I would speak back. Most of the time they would have a certain look in their eyes. A look of uncertainty or curiosity could be seen in their eyes. Most people are cruel to disabled people. I have been stared at for long periods of time. I have been laughed at and even called names by strangers. But I always tried to stay positive and respectful with self-control. I often wondered why people laugh at people born with disabilities. Sometimes it is the most painful and hurtful act any person can commit. Some people are so cruel to the less fortunate.

Well, one weekend at the mall Angel was talking to this girl and I was just sitting in my wheelchair admiring things and looking around. I was positioned next to a row of payphones when one starting ringing. There were three pretty young Latin girls walking by at the same time. All of a sudden one of them ran over and answered the phone. Her friends ran behind her laughing and giggling. Out the corner of my eyes I noticed the girls were having fun talking to whoever was on the phone. They passed the phone from one to another as they laughed and smiled non-stop. After about

49

five minutes one of the girls hung the phone up and they all ran away laughing uncontrollably. At that moment a thought crossed my mind and I pulled out a pen and copied every number off every payphone there. My mind was running 100 mile per hour as I thought I couldn't wait until I got home. Maybe I could get lucky and get a girl to answer one of the phones if I called it. Whoever was on that previous call sure had those girls going for about five minutes. I figured if I could just get a female to answer the phone I could at least have a phone conversation with a girl without her looking at me like I had two heads.

That night at my house I called number after number. I would call one number and let it ring about ten times than call another. I wasn't having any luck just people picking up the phone and hanging up. Sometimes they would pick up the phone and say hello and then say something stupid or just curse and hang up. After about an hour I was getting frustrated and tired and decided it was a stupid idea. I decided to give up and go to bed. But for some reason I couldn't stop thinking about how those girl had responded to that call. I couldn't shake the thought from my mind. I went to sleep with it on my mind and wondering should I try again the next day.

When I woke up the next morning all I could think about was what time the mall would be opening and all the girls that would be walking by those payphones. I didn't tell my mother what I was doing or even Angel. I didn't want to seem desperate. I just wanted to hear the soft sound of a female on the other end of a phone. I wanted to hold a conversation with a female who couldn't see this damn wheelchair. I wanted to feel whole and talk to girls like guys my age did. I mean I wasn't a little kid anymore. I might have weighed as much as a little boy but I wasn't a little boy. I was in my late teens now and I wanted to date and more, if possible. Maybe I was overreacting but I didn't care it was my life. It was time for me to do things I wanted to do by any means necessary.

As soon as eleven o'clock came I began dialing the numbers. I knew the mall opened at ten and that by eleven it would be getting crowed. After about thirty minutes my doorbell rang. It was Angel and he wanted to know what time I was coming out. He asked me what I was doing. At first I was reluctant to tell him. Then I figured what the hell. So I told him I was calling the payphones at the mall. Angel was a trouper all he said was let me try next. We laughed as we called one number after another. Then we broke luck after about twenty minutes. We got two females on the phone and we were taking turns talking to them. They were from Ringwood, New Jersey. They were Puerto Rican girls just hanging out in the mall. One name was Amy and the other one name was Marie. We talked to them for hours on the phone that day. It was a dream come true and the

51

beginning of a beautiful friendship. We exchanged numbers with them and began talking to them every day. Now Angel was talking to Amy first but somehow I and Amy just seemed to hit it off better. We talked on the phone everyday every chance we got. Amy and I became very close. It was a telephone relationship but it was fine with me. I never told her about my disabilities I figured I'd deal with that when the time came.

At this time my friends and I began to hang in front of my grandmother's building where she lived. I stayed with her most of the time because her apartment was more handicapped accessible for me. Even though there was just a fence that separated my mother apartment from my grandmothers. I was hanging with Angel and the crew all the time now. I felt certain realness now because I had a telephone girlfriend in Amy. I don't know what it was but we just hit it off immediately. I guess there were things she was missing in her life too. I know I was missing things I needed a friend of the opposite sex. We would talk for hours and hours on the phone. Being from Ringwood she was more like a Valley Girl.

At this time somebody introduced me to a new world, a world of chat line. Chat line was called the "Raven." You could call the chat line and meet people from all over the world. Between hanging with Angel and talking on the chat lines and Amy my life was really becoming natural and real.

My Mom Vicky

I don't know who invented chat lines but it was better than food to me.

Chapter 11

The more Amy and I talked on the phone the closer we became. We seemed to hit it off immediately. She was beginning to fall in love with me even though we had never met. I guess I just knew the right things to say at the right time in her life. Females loved to talk and most of the time they just wanted someone to listen. And believe me I had nothing but time to listen, where was I going. Also with Amy being a Valley Girl from Ringwood, she fell quickly for the street dialogue that I spoke.

I began to feel funny and grow tired of the chat lines. Amy was consuming most of my time. The chat lines were great and you could meet a lot of people from all over the world, but Amy and I had a certain connection. Chat lines are very useful for people in need of meeting other people when your self-esteem was low. They were also good if you didn't think you looked handsome or pretty enough for someone else. On chat lines, you could be whoever you wanted to when you want to.

After several weeks of conversations on the phone with Amy, the urge to meet her grew more and more intense. Even though I was the one in the wheelchair it seemed as if she had something to hide too. I wondered was she handicapped too. Was she hiding something behind her soft and sexy voice? She had described herself to me several times. She claimed to have long hair with a soft bright Latin complexion. Amy claimed to be very thick and chunky but not overweight. I also had described everything about myself except one small thing. I never told her about my wheelchair and my disease. Every time we talked I swear I wanted to, but I would never exactly mention it.

Amy was becoming more and more in love with my voice and my conversation. I believe we became as close as any two people could get that only talked on the phone. It had a certain type of sexy feeling that only people who have ever had telephone love can explain. I guess it's the element of the unknown that attracted people to certain people, places, and things. We had become so close that it had a certain air of danger to it.

After several more weeks of talking on the phone it was time for the big showdown. Angel had become close with one of Amy friends. They also held a telephone relationship like Amy and I. I don't think they were as serious and close as we were, but they were casual acquaintances. Amy and I were beyond that. We were in love. Even though we had never even met we were in love. And it all began from a simple phone call to a payphone.

My mother and grandmother were aware of my new profound telephone love and were pleased and happy for me.

55

Over time Angel and I had begun to hang out in front of my grandmother's apartment building with the other boys. This seemed to drive the tenants in the building crazy. They began to make complaints to the higher ups. My grandmother didn't care at all as far as she was concerned her little "Dre" could do no wrong.

One day while talking to Amy she finally agreed to meet me at the mall. It was time and the stage was set. Angel and I would meet Amy and her friend at Burger King in the Garden State Plaza mall. For some reason even though I had never told her about my wheelchair, I wasn't afraid or scared. We had talked too much on the phone. She had told me she loved me over a thousand times. Amy had promised no matter what I looked like it didn't matter because she was in the love with "Dre" the loving and caring and poetic voice on the phone. Did I have little doubts? Of course I did. I'm human. But I had to give it a shot. I needed to know if someone could love me for me. Could someone understand my disability and my flaws?

On the bus with Angel I grew more and more fidgety the closer we got to the mall. I noticed Angel wasn't his usual cool and calm and collective self either. I wondered what was on his mind. Angel was a player with the capital "P". Deep down inside I knew what was eating away at Angel. He knew that I didn't let Amy know I was in a wheelchair and he was concerned for my feelings. I told him to loosen up and that everything would be alright. Whatever happens happens.

When the bus stopped at the mall it felt like my heart was doing the hustle inside my chest. For one quick instinct I thought about turning around and getting right back on the bus. But I had come too far and waited too long for this moment. Either she would like me or not. I thought to myself, *what could be the worst thing that could happen? She would talk to me and then tell me I'm not what she was looking for. She would look at me and laugh. Would she walk right by me and not even mumble one word.* My mind was racing when we reached Burger King. About fifteen minutes before our prearranged time, Angel and I waited right where we told them we would be. We had told them what we would have on and they had told us what they were wearing. Angel and I made small talk for about ten minutes and there was about five minutes left. For one quick moment I hoped they wouldn't show. The pressure and the anticipation were rising to a peak. Each minute seemed like an eternity.

The noticed Angel body jerk erect. His head did a double take and then he nudged me. My eyes followed his eyes. There they were two Latin females walking in our direction. I spotted Amy right away and somehow I just knew it was her. She was a little overweight but she was beautiful. And she did look like Pocahontas. Her hair was long down her back and she had bedroom eyes. Her girlfriend was very attractive too. She was small and well put together. She kind of reminded me of a Indian princess. They still hadn't spotted us yet. I could tell by the way their heads were turning back and forth. They were just walking and talking and laughing. I told Angel that they don't even see us over here.

As they walked around the Burger King looking for me and Angel it dawned on me. They didn't recognize us because they were looking for two guys. They weren't looking for one guy standing and another in a wheelchair. As they circled the store again this time they headed straight for Angel and me. I never felt so much pressure in my whole life. And then it happened. They were standing about six feet away when I called out to her.

"Amy. Amy, it's me, Dre." They stopped right in their tracks. We were so close to each other we could have shook hands. I repeated, "Amy, it's me, Dre." They were still standing there frozen in time. It seemed like forever as they stood there staring at me. I tried to crack a little smile to break the ice. Then Amy and her friend looked at each other and then looked at me again. They looked at me for one quick second. Then they looked at each other one more time and burst out into laughter. They turned around and in a flash they ran like hell out of the Burger King, still laughing. People turned and watched as they did the one hundred yard dash away from me. My whole body went numb and I felt sick to my stomach. All I wanted to do was get back on that bus and get back to Paterson as quick as I could.

Angel tried his best to cheer me up. He told me that they weren't worth it anyway. He called them a million names over and over. But everything he said fell on deaf ears. My heart had been crushed and there was nothing anyone could say or do to help me. I cursed the world for being born with Muscular Dystrophy. I cursed the world for having a tracheostomy. I pounded my hand against my wheelchair until my hand burned like fire. I was done trying to be like everyone else. I was done trying to meet girls. It wasn't the end of the world but let me tell you it felt like it.

Why did this have to happen to me? I told my mother about the whole thing. Once again she was there with kind words and wisdom. "Listen, Andre, there is somebody in the world for everybody, believe me. You may be hurting right now and trust me you won't be the first or the last to have your heart broken. But I promise you one day you will find love and it's going to be when you least expect it. You will find someone to love you for you. Love comes in many shapes, forms and fashions. I know nothing I can say can make you feel better right now, but one day you going to tell me I was right." She was right. There was nothing she could say that could make me feel better. My heart was broken and my spirit was crushed. I felt empty and worthless inside. No matter what I tried to do I couldn't shake it. Over and over my mind kept replaying the events. All I could see was Amy and her friend hauling ass away from me as fast as they could.

After the first day I thought the pain would ease up a little. I was wrong. The pain got worse with every minute that passed. Whoever said that time heals all wounds was far from true. My pain was as strong as ever and I couldn't see any relief coming anytime soon. I picked up the phone over and over to called Amy but every time I would just hang the receiver back up. Sometimes I would dial one digit and hung up and sometimes I would get as far as six digits and then hang up. I still remember the second day after it happened. Wishing I didn't have to wait up for the third day. The first two days had been too hard and depressing. Angel was trying to get me to shake it and also my mom. I didn't even feel like chilling in front of my grandmother's building with Angel and the boys. I was a complete mess and everyone close to me knew it.

Chapter 12

It was the third day since my life was turned upside down by Amy. I woke up and wished I could have slept longer. In fact I didn't give a damn if I slept forever. What could I do to shake this feeling in my heart? The pain was unbearable. It was beginning to feel like I couldn't make it pass the next minute.

As I lay in bed tears began to roll down my face to my chin. Before I knew it tears were rolling backward into my ears. The sheets on my bed under my head began to get wet from my uncontrollable waterfall of tears. I heard my grandmother outside my room so I tried hard to control the tears and the inside grief I was feeling. I knew as hard as I tried to hide my pain it was still be visible on my face.

Around noon I decided that I couldn't lie in bed any longer. I pulled my wheelchair close to the bed and lifted myself into my chair. Before I made my exit out of my bedroom I tried to fix my face to hide the pain I felt inside. I went into the bathroom to freshen up a little and brush my teeth. While I was brushing my teeth I took a long hard look at myself. I was lost in a trance and trying to figure out why me. I began to second-guess my future and well-being. Maybe Amy was right for running away from me. Maybe it

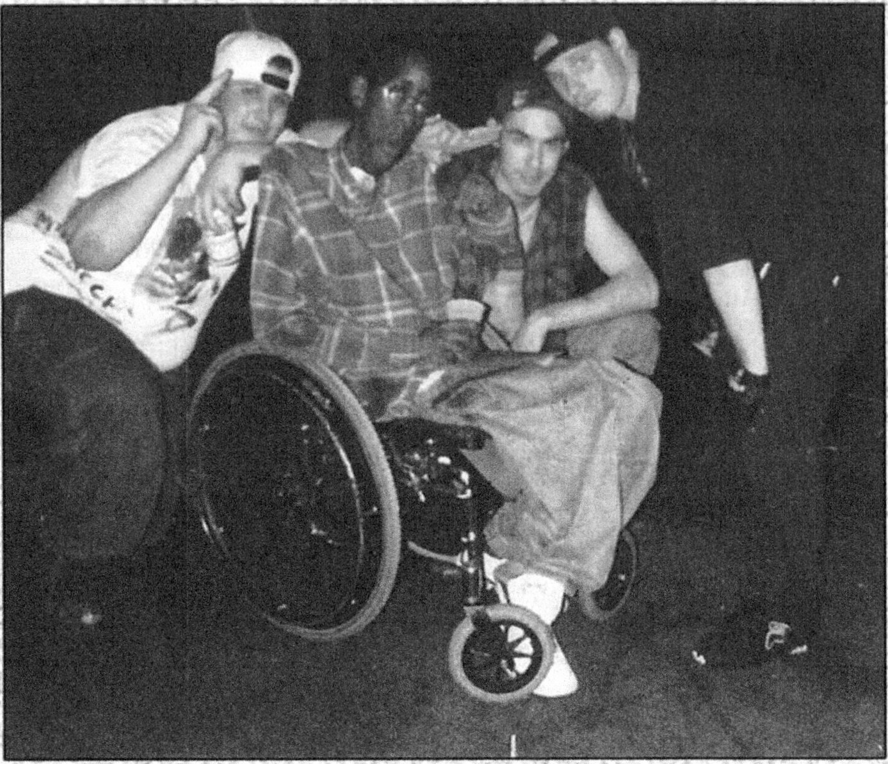

Wally, Me, Chase and Chance

was not only too much for her to handle but any young girl her age. My mind was playing tricks on me. I would curse Amy out and then the world. I was still stuck in a trance in the bathroom staring at myself in the mirror. I ask God over and over again why I had to be born like this. WHY ME, GOD? WHY ME, DAD? WHY ME, MOM? WHY? WHY? WHY? WHY?

I was stuck in a trance for what seemed like hours. And then my trance was broken by the screams of my grandmother yelling my name over and over again. But I was so caught up in the daydream it sounded like the screams were coming from miles away. I couldn't break the trance I was in. If you ever been sleep and having a nightmare but couldn't wakeup you know what I mean then. Finally my grandmother came to the bathroom door and yelled, "Andre, don't you hear me calling you boy? I had been calling your name for about five minute's boy." I turned and looked at my grandmother and told her I'm sorry. She shook her head and handed me the telephone and turned around and walked away.

I placed my finger over the hole in the front of my neck and whisper into the receiver, "Hello." Then I spoke a little louder into the phone, "Hello." At that time I heard the best sounds I had heard in the last three days. The soft and sexy voice on the other end of the phone was none other than Amy. It was Amy. All at once my heart starting pounding and I began to sweat like I had just finished a marathon, a handicap marathon of course. I quickly wheeled myself back into my room and closed the door behind me.

My mind was racing as I held the phone to my ear and listened to her speak. Amy went on and on about how sorry she was for doing the one hundred yard dash away from me that day. She would go on to say it was too much for her to handle at one time. She also said that she didn't know how to deal with a situation like that because it caught her off guard. She was afraid, scared, and caught totally by surprise. I tried to cut in and explain to her that it was ok, but before I could finish she cut me off and told me to just listen.

Amy went on to say, "Andre, I'm very, very sorry about running away from you at the mall like that. But ever since that day, my life has been missing something and that something is you. At first I had so many mixed emotion and feelings. I couldn't eat and I couldn't sleep. Every minute of the day my mind kept playing back that intense moment at the mall when I first saw you. We had become so close on the phone. We had become more than friends, we were companions, soul-mates, partners. We were one as a whole and we needed each other every day even if it was on the phone. I realize that I could not go on and leave this situation like this. Andre, I want you and need you in my life. Andre, I love you and if you accept my sincere apology, I will never hurt you again. I don't care about the wheelchair. I love you, the man I fell in love with on the telephone. Call me crazy, call me stupid, but one thing I know is what my heart wants and that's you Andre Williams."

The whole time she was speaking I just held the phone frozen in time. My mind went back to the days when I could walk, Wally, grand and great-grandparents and even my mom. My whole life flashed in front of me as she talked and talked and talked. I guess at that time nothing else mattered to me. I finally found someone to love me for me. I thought this day would never come. All the days and nights I cried inside wondering why me, God, why me. And here the day was. If I didn't say I was a little unprepared for the bombshell I would be lying.

After she finally stopped talking it was like we never missed a beat. We talked on the phone that day for hours and hours. I held on while she took a shower and she held on while I went to the bathroom. It seemed like we never hung the phone up for the next month. It was the best month of my life. Amy and I became closer every minute of every day. But there was one thing that was driving me crazy. It was the one thing that drives every young teenage boy crazy. I was still a virgin. On the other hand, to say driving me crazy was an understatement, it was *killing* me.

I really don't want to brag about this but I guess when God took my legs away he blessed me in another area. How can I say this, I'm really well hung. Yes, I'm blessed and well-endowed. And it was definitely time for me to lose my virginity and pop a cherry.

Chapter 13

After a month of phone conversation everyday non-stop, we decided it was time for some face-to- face. So we got the bus schedule together and set a date. Now this was where the problems began. One, Amy lived in Ringwood, New Jersey, and would have to take two New Jersey Transit buses to get to the mall. As for me it was also a few obstacles to overcome. First of all, at this time whenever a person in a wheelchair wanted to ride public transportation, you would have to call the bus company and fill them in with the time and bus stop you would be at. Also you would have to give them your ending destination and return time if needed. For some reason when the bus finally got there it seemed as if NATO was about to launch a rocket into orbit. And the passengers on the bus wouldn't handle the launching any better. If you're curious about what I'm talking about and never had the opportunity of witnessing a launching of a human satellite allow me to enlighten you.

First, you have to make sure you're at the plan pick-up spot at least thirty minutes ahead of time. Because God-forbid you miss the bus assigned you were screwed. If the next bus coming wasn't assigned to pick up a wheelchair passenger holy hell would break out. So the bus driver would have to pull-up as close to the curb as possible and extend the carrier out and lower it. Then I would have to roll my wheelchair onto the carrier and lock my wheels. Then the bus driver would hit another button to raise me up to the bus floor level and draw me inward. This is where it gets more interesting. The front passenger seat which might hold anywhere from 4 to 5 people was where I was to be locked in.

So let me remind you that from the time the bus pulled up and announced to all the passengers that they would be there for about 5 minutes picking up a handicapped passenger everyone grew impatient. So everyone on the left side of bus would be staring out the bus window, while all the passengers seated on the right side of the bus would stand up and try their damn best to watch this circus event. I felt like the bus driver was the Ring Master and I was the show while all the passengers were the audience. How insensitive people were to the handicapped. Now the bus driver would have to inform anyone sitting on the front couch seat to please find another seat because that was where handicapped people were locked in. God-forbid if the bus was crowed and they had to find another seat. So after the bus driver lifted up the front couch seat and locked me in and finally began on his journey again, the nasty and twisted stares and whispers would also begin. And lo and behold the worst thing about this was when I reached the mall he would have to do the whole procedure all over again but in reverse. This was also for my return as well.

All and all with Amy having to take two buses and me having to be launched into orbit four times; it was nothing because our love had become so strong. Now this part might seem a little crazy but every weekend we would do all this just to spend 15 or 20 minutes with each other. The reason being was with Amy living in Ringwood and the bus schedule not being as regular as needed we were only together about 15 minutes every visit. So after about two months of this it was about time for us to spend more time with each other. My mother was having a big cookout and I planned on inviting Amy to come down. So after well planning and many conversations it was set. Amy would come to my mother's cookout and bring a girlfriend for Angel.

Wow. I couldn't believe we were finally going to be able to spend time together. Also I had spoken to my mother about wanting to have sex on a couple of occasions. She was cool with me using her apartment to lose my virginity. Angel and I talked about the cookout and the girls coming down from Ringwood all the time. At this time in my life I was becoming one horny little handicapped kid. Handicap or not I needed to get laid. Wheelchair and tracheostomy meant nothing to the weight of my balls; I needed to release in the worst way. Playing with myself no longer carried any effect

Grandmother and Mom

Life

L

Humble

Ent.

H

Dre

ENT.

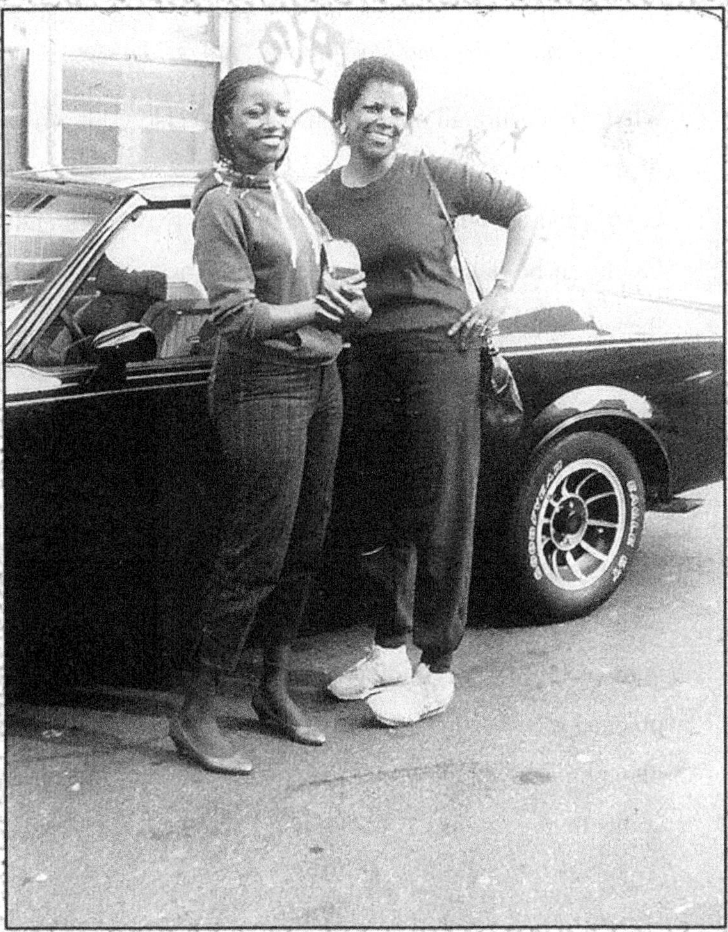

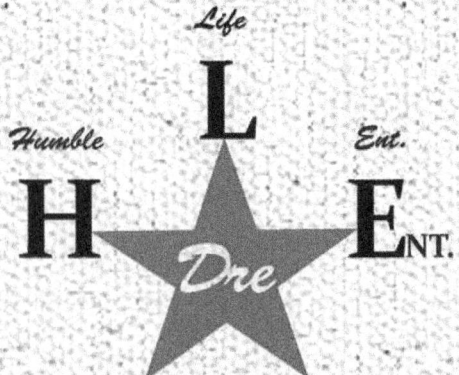

on me. I needed to feel the warm wet tunnel inside a woman's vagina.

So the day had finally come and the stage was set. Amy and her girlfriend were on the bus on their way to Paterson from Ringwood. The cookout was in full swing when they finally arrived. My mother and everyone made sure Amy and her friend felt right at home. It was one of the best cookout's I had ever attended. I had a girlfriend and it felt great to be seen with a woman who was with me and only me for the world to see. Amy never left my side the whole time she was there. And even though Angel had a girlfriend he still was trying his best to get in Amy's girlfriend pants. When I heard Luther Vandross song "The Night I Fell in Love" I knew it was time for me to make my move. I told Amy to excuse me for a minute as I powered my wheelchair over to my mother. Oh yeah, just in case I didn't mention this before, I received a motored wheelchair at fifteen years old. And the strange thing is I never have felt handicap unless my powered wheelchair was broke.

I told my mom that Angel and I and Amy and her friend were going to go inside her apartment and chill for a little while, before it was time for her bus to come. I winked at my mom to seal the deal before I powered my chair back over to Amy. So we all went into my mom's house. The only thing that was on my mind was sex. Once inside we began smoking marijuana. I could tell that this was going to be the day when I finally got laid. Even though I only weight about 60 pounds and had never told Amy I had a tracheostomy in my neck I felt confident. I knew Amy loved me and it didn't matter if I was a two-headed, four-legged bull frog.

Angel didn't waste any time. He was making a fake bed on the floor in the corner for Amy's friend and him to lie down on. When I saw them lie down and get under the covers I knew it was time for me to make my move. I moved as close to the bed as possible and lifted myself from my chair onto the bed. I got under the covers and pulled my pants down to my knees. My penis was as hard as a rock. Amy was still standing up looking at me and then her friend in the corner under the sheets with Angel. She suddenly walked around to the other side of the bed and got into the bed fully dressed. She got under the covers and pulled the covers up to her neck. Now, Amy was Hispanic but very pretty with long hair. She was a little chubby but still attractive. I guessed she was a little shy about her weight but it meant nothing to me because she was beautiful. She began to undress. Suddenly I had a thought that this was a dream come true. I was about to lose my virginity to a beautiful Hispanic Valley Girl from Ringwood, New Jersey. Some African-American brothers go a lifetime and never even kiss a Latin girl. *Damn*, I thought to myself. *I should have suctioned my tracheostomy out.* I could feel my lungs feeling up with fluid. But so be it, I didn't care if there was an

70

earthquake coming I wasn't about to stop this from happening. If I died I figured I would die on top of a beautiful girl. I had waited for this moment my whole life.

When she was finally undressed I started rubbing on her stomach. I was working my way up to her breasts. I wanted one of them things in my mouth in the worst way. Her skin was soft liked silk or butter. As I played with her breasts I started rubbing her nipples and all of a sudden it happened. She went under the covers and grabbed my penis and started licking it. Now this was the first time I ever received a blowjob so pardon me if I seem a bit childish. But when she put my penis in her mouth it felt like something exploded inside my body. I thought I blacked out and came to. I closed my eyes and for some reason I was "Michael Jordan" gliding from the foul line doing that famous "Dr. J" jam at the dunk contest. Out of the corner of my eye I thought I saw Angel leaving the room. Then I thought I heard a female crying but I was still gliding through the air like Michael Jordan. Suddenly Amy stopped and I soared back down to reality. Amy's girlfriend was crying because Angel had broken the record on the quickest orgasm ever known to man, and then bolted out the room like Flash Gordon.

Amy jumped out of bed and wrapped herself in a sheet and quickly ran over to her friend to console her. Now being handicapped definitely taught me how to show sympathy for other people's feelings. But this had happened at the wrong time. I mean damn! Really now while I was getting oral sex for the first time and about to lose my virginity. Now I don't know what happened between Angel and the girlfriend. Did Angel come too fast and the embarrassment was too much for his manhood to handle? Did she have a bad odor or bad breath? Maybe Angel couldn't get it up. Was she almost there and Angel couldn't hold his? I didn't have the slightest idea but all I was thinking was bitch, don't kill my vibe.

After maybe ten minutes Angel returned to the room. They began talking again. And Amy returned back to bed. Amy was trying to tell me what happened but to be honest I can't remember one word she said to this day. All I wanted to do was continue right where we left off. The hard-on I had didn't miss a beat; my penis was still standing up like a rattle snake head. After she gave it a couple of more licks I was ready for the main course. Now being that Amy was thick and I only weighed about 50 to 60 pounds we had to position ourselves just right. Remember Muscular Dystrophy affects your muscles in your shoulders, face and most important the pelvis. Now you know I was going to need my hips to push forward and pull backwards.

So Amy lies on her back and I straddled her kind of like in a frog position. In the meantime Angel left the room again but this time Amy friend handled it like a pro. I guess she didn't want to be a labeled cock blocker. So as I pushed myself up to the best of my ability in a frog position Amy grabbed my penis and tried to put it in her vagina. But for some reason I couldn't find the forbidden fruit. My penis would feel the wetness and the lips and then slide to the right or to the left. After several attempts I began to wonder if this was foreplay for her. If it was, it damn sure wasn't for me. Angel had been gone for about 15 to 20 minutes now. I guess Amy's friend was enjoying the show and maybe even playing with herself. Then all of a sudden I hit the jackpot. Amy placed my penis right smack in the middle of her vagina and I felt the warmth inside of her tunnel wrapped around my penis head like a glove. She was on the bottom but she would have to push up and down to rock my body up and down. With every push up I felt my penis enter her warm wet tunnel a little more. My body felt like it had been blown into a million pieces. It was really happening, I was having sex and the feeling was unbelievable.

As the aroma of sex filled my nose with a beautiful fragrance, I closed my eyes and smiled from ear to ear. When my penis head was just a little pass the inside of her vagina lips, she began to push upward with a strong thrust. Her eyes were closed and she was breathing heavy like she was maybe taken her last breath. She was saying over and over again, "Oh Papi! Oh Papi! Oh Papi!" I was on my elbows as she rocked me back and forth, up and down. It was poetry in motion and our chemistry was just about perfect. And then Amy placed her palms flat on the bed on both sides of her body for better leverage. At that moment she gave one big push upwards and I felt my penis sliding in deeper. Then all of a sudden we heard a loud crashing sound and then a thump. It came from outside the window. We all froze and then looked at the window, then at each other, and then back at the window. Amy and her girlfriend ran over to the window and pulled the blinds up. Then they looked at each other and back out the window and then at me. I screamed, "What happen?" Amy and her girlfriend began to laugh uncontrollably. It was Angel and he was lying flat out on his back. He was trying to watch Amy and me through the window and fell down the fire escape.

Of all the times Angel had decided to become a peeping tom he picked that day. That was the last straw for Amy. She got dressed and just like that my first experience with sex ended like that. No orgasm, no cuddling, no happy ending would come out of this. Angel single handily destroyed my first encounter. Amy whispered in my ear, "Don't worry, baby, because from now on we'll be alone when we get together." And with that said I couldn't do anything but wait and trust and believe my pretty, sexy Latin Pocahontas.

Chapter 14

After that day I made sure that nothing like that would ever happen again. When Amy came to see me she was alone and the time we spend together was ours. I don't have to get into every detail but let's just say from that day on it was nothing but good times. Now don't get me wrong, Amy was a virgin too when I met her, but she was no stranger to giving head. I guess she was a little ashamed of her weight. So it was a case of the blind leading the blind. I introduced her to marijuana. So we would smoke and then get in the bed and get it on. And so that's how our relationship went for years. We were soul mates to the end.

Amy taught me to have self-esteem and confidence. She would always make me feel like I was just as good as any man with two legs. Amy taught me to see beyond my wheelchair and disabilities. And that's why I love her even to this day. Amy was my Valley Girl who embraced me and loved me like I needed to be loved. She touched me the way I needed to be touched. And she was there for me the way a woman should be there for her man. And I was there for her the way a man should be there for his women. Till deaths do us part was our motto.

One day Amy convinced me to come up to Ringwood

with her to chill. Even though she knew her parents were against her dealing with an African-American man, she didn't give a damn. I was very hesitant about this idea. She explained to me that her parents would be at work. So after days of contemplating the situation I decided to go. After countless buses and aggravation, I finally made it there. Ringwood, New Jersey, looked like another planet to me. When I finally made it to her house it was like a dream. Amy had a sister and both of their rooms were on the top floors in their parents' house. Now this is where the story gets gangster. Amy sister had her boyfriend living upstairs with her and her parents never even had a hint. So I guess Amy thought it was her time to try and pull the wool over her parent's eyes and sneak me in.

When I entered the house it was a real mansion type house. Amy called her sister and her sister called her boyfriend. This dude carried me up the stairs into Amy's room. These two sisters were far from daddy's little girls. Well, one day turned to two and two turned to three and before I knew it I had been at Amy's house for about two weeks. I stayed in her room and her parents never even had a clue. Now every day Amy would go to school and I would just stay there and lie in bed and watch TV. After about a week and a half I began to feel comfortable and right a home.

So after about two weeks Amy kissed me goodbye and

left for school. But for some reason I just had a funny feeling in my gut that morning. Amy's father had caught her sister's boyfriend in her room about three days ago and I was still shook about that. Amy assured me that I didn't have anything to worry about. So about two hours after Amy had left for school I heard her door open. I was so quiet. I wasn't even breathing. It was Amy's father and he was cleaning up her room. Now I was so small he couldn't tell I was in the bed. I was maybe fifty-five pounds at the most. My heart was pounding so hard I thought he would hear it. I laid there motionless like a dead corpse. In my mind I pleaded with God for him to hurry up and leave. I was positioned on the edge of the bed. Then all of a sudden he walked over to the bed where I was laying. He still couldn't see me under the covers. Suddenly he sat down on the bed right on top of me. We both screamed at the same time. He snatched the covers back and stared at me laying there in my birthday suit. His eyes opened so wide you could have read his mind. His face went from shocked to angry in a split second. Then his eyes sent a special delivery message to me and the message spelled out MURDER.

He bolted out the room screaming in Spanish. I didn't understand what he was saying but I was sure it wasn't anything kind. I could hear him running back up the stairs still screaming in Spanish. So I started screaming too. I kept yelling over and over again, "I can't walk! I can't walk! I can't walk!" All of a sudden he busted the door open and was holding a baseball bat over his head. I began to point at my legs and screamed louder, "I'm crippled! I'm crippled. I'm crippled. Please, please don't hit me."

Right before he bashed my skull in, he stopped and looked at my small frame. We were locked in time for what seemed like minutes. Then like a ghost he turned and ran out the room. I laid there soak and wet from sweating with fear. About forty-five minutes later I heard Amy. She was screaming at the top of her lungs. Amy was yelling at her father for going into her room. They were having a heated argument and it was loud. Here Amy was sixteen years old and hiding a man from Paterson in her bedroom behind her parents back. And after all that she had done she still stood her ground like she hadn't done anything wrong. Amy was indeed a Valley Girl gangster from Ringwood, New Jersey.

Needless to say, Paterson never looked so good when I finally got back home.

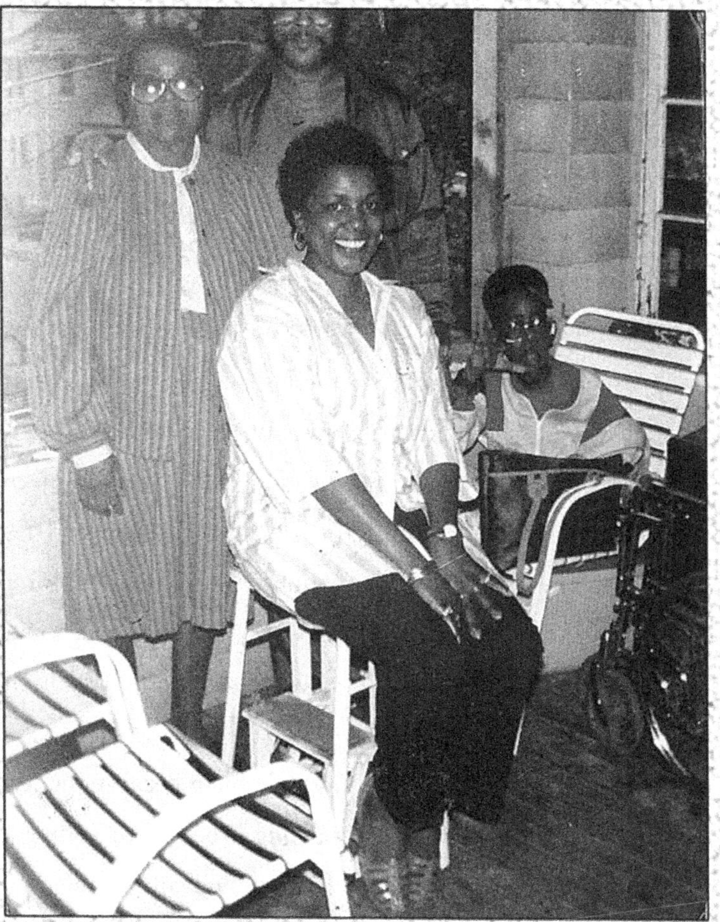

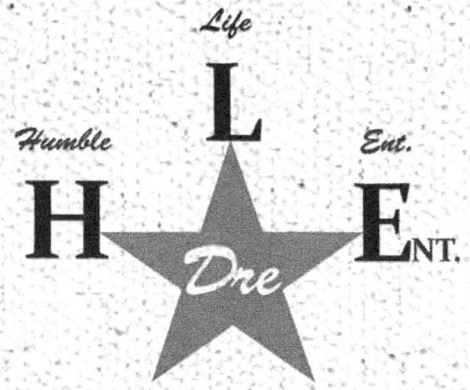

Grandmom, Great Grandmom and Andre

Chapter 15

Time was flying by and Amy and I had been together two years already. It had been nothing but good times and fun. I guess God had made Amy just for me. She loved me and I loved her very much. I guess now that I was doing grown man things I felt like a grown man. So whenever I wasn't with Amy or on the phone with her, I was chilling in front of my grandmother's apartment with Angel and the boys. We would hang out there and smoke and joke all day until the early hours of the night.

I guess we were becoming a problem because the tenants and neighbors started complaining. They were getting tired of us hanging in front of the building all the time. So it wasn't too long before the superintendent and owner starting complaining to my grandmother about my friends and me. Why they decided to pick me as the ringleader I never understood. Out of all of us that hung out in front of that damn building they wanted to blame the kid in the wheelchair. Maybe they thought if I wouldn't come outside and sit in front of the building then nobody else would.

So the tenants complained to the Super and the Super complained to the Owner and the Owner complained to the Housing Authority. Then all hell broke loose when the

Housing Authority straight out told my grandmother they wanted me out of her apartment. Can you believe that? They told my grandmother either I get out or she would have to move out!

I guess the Housing Authority underestimated my grandmother and that old fashion toughness. My grandmother told them that her grandson wasn't going anywhere. She also gave them a few choice words as she gave them a giant piece of her mind. My great-grandmother was born in 1920. And if she didn't let the cotton fields of North Carolina and Jim Crow laws scare her, then the Housing Authority was sure wasting their good old time.

Things went on as usual for a while after that. Amy and I was still a major item. Angel and I and the boys were still hanging in front of grandma's building every day. It was just something to do, somewhere to chill and hangout. But if you know Paterson, then you know your business will soon become everybody's business. And this I couldn't understand at that time in my life.

One morning Amy called me and told me she wasn't feeling well. She couldn't keep anything on her stomach. Every morning when she would wakeup she would have to throw up. She assumed she was just coming down with a cold or something. Then she began to think that maybe it was just a stomach virus. With my great-grandmother being pressured to put me out or move, and Amy being sick all the time, it was all starting to take a toll on me.

Then one day all hell broke loose when my great-grandmother received a phone call about me having to leave the premises. My grandmother was giving housing a tongue lashing on the phone. But all I remember was the last thing she said. "I'm moving out of this building because my grandson isn't leaving anywhere, and I'm not making him leave either." And just like that it was done, we were moving. My granny wasn't letting anybody tell her to put me out of nowhere.

One week after that I was hit with another bombshell. This would be one of the biggest news flashes I had ever received in my whole life. It sent me on a one-way ride to manhood, maturity and fatherhood. Amy called me and asked me could I talk. Of course I could talk and listen and reply. She hesitated and kept beating around the bush. I was growing more and more impatient by the second. And then she said, "Andre, I'm pregnant." I thought I heard what she said but I wasn't sure. So I said, "You're what?" "Andre, I'm having your baby. I'm pregnant."

So right then and there time had stopped. I was stuck and trying to really understand what Amy was saying. I was going to be a father. Then all of a sudden a fear came over me like never before. I had been through an operation, coma, loss of voice, medical procedures, and in and out of doctors' offices and hospitals. But until that day I had never felt so afraid of anything. But when Amy told me I was going to be a father, it scared me beyond belief.

I didn't know what to do or who to tell, so I didn't tell anybody. On the other hand, Amy was just as scared as I was. As a matter of fact it would be eight months before we told anybody or anybody even found out she was having a baby.

Three weeks had gone by when my great-grandmother told me she found another apartment for us and that included my mom. We were moving and not just anywhere but to the projects, Alabama Ave Projects aka "The Pound." Between Amy being pregnant and the news of moving into the projects my head was spinning. Even though I had grown up in Paterson, the projects were a different world. And trust me if you thought I was afraid to be a father, multiply that fear times one million. I, Andre Williams the little handicap disabled kid in the wheelchair moving into the projects. I must have asked my granny thousand times why we had to move into the projects. Between Amy being pregnant and moving into the projects I was a nervous wreck. I was very, very, very scared. But Granny was a soldier. She didn't try to hear me out or understand where I was coming from. It was a done deal. Fatherhood and the projects were in my immediate future. I couldn't do anything to prevent either one! Those two events would set my life up for some of the biggest heartaches I would ever come to know. On the other hand, I would get the knowledge of street education and life that I could have never learned at any top colleges in the world in ten life times.

Chapter 16

June 18, 1997, that date shall forever be locked in my heart, my mind, and my soul. On this day in my life a miracle happened. This was and always will be one of the happiest days of my life. It was the day my first-born, my son came into this world. Raymond Vicent Williams, born eight pounds and thirteen ounces. Raymond had thick eyelashes, dark eyes, curly black hair and a small button shaped nose. He was the cutest baby I had ever seen. I was so caught up in the moment when I reached the hospital it never even crossed my mind to ask was he healthy. I didn't care about anything but seeing and holding my son. God had really blessed us with a beautiful baby, and he was 100% healthy. When I heard those words it made my whole world complete. I had always heard that girls were rarely born with Muscular Dystrophy. So I was on edge until I received the final verdict from the doctor. "HEALTHY, HEALTHY, HEALTHY," I shouted over and over again.

Time was flying by and it seemed like my life was moving so fast. Amy's family after taking her pregnancy so hard fell hooked, lined and sinker in love with Raymond. They had practically taken full control over raising our son. Whenever Amy came to visit me she was not allowed to bring Raymond. Her parents felt that if she brought Raymond to Paterson they would never see him again. Paterson was the ghetto to them. As far as they were concerned it was no place for a little baby to be.

Months would go by without me even seeing my son at all. I guessed I had to put myself in their shoes; they had already loss Amy to the streets of Paterson. They for damn sure weren't going to let their first grandson even get a whiff of Paterson air. But at that time in my life I was so consumed with getting laid and smoking weed that I figured maybe them keeping him sheltered wasn't all that bad.

The move to the projects was finally complete. It was as official as a referee with a whistle. We had our date to move into the projects and it was quickly approaching. I had so many thoughts running through my mind. Here I was a handicapped kid in a wheelchair moving into the projects. Over and over I thought to myself that the hardships would be plenty. I tried my best to keep my optimism high. But everywhere I went I would hear the same things: "Andre, you're going to get beat up." "Andre, you're going to get robbed." "Andre this, and Andre that." My friends had my head spinning from all the horror stories they were telling me. If I knew then, what I know now, I would have told them all to, "Kiss my handicap ass!" None of them had never even walked into the projects let alone lived there!

During the waiting process for the big move my mother

had hit a relationship jackpot. She met a tall handsome dark-skinned man from Africa. My mother had indeed met a real Mandingo man. Everything about him was gracious, from his accent to his mannerism. Before him my mother was on a slight spiral down. She had begun to use drugs. I wasn't exactly sure what she was using but I knew it was something.

She was definitely changing, and we all could see it. And then she met her prince charming. I called him "The African Savior" because he helped save my mother's life.

They moved to Jersey City, New Jersey, and were doing great. My mother even got her driver's license. Then he bought her a car because he loved her so much. Man it felt good to see my mother pulling up in her own car. She had been through so many bad relationships. It seemed like one after another she just couldn't find the right man. So when I say my family and I were happy for her I mean it from the bottom of my heart.

It kind of bothered me that she wouldn't be moving into the projects with granny and me, but hey, she was happy. And if she was happy I was happy with her situation. So it looked like it would just be my great-grandmother and me against the world.

Amy's parents had bought her a car and she was brushing up on her skills before she took that long ride down Route 23 to Route 80 into Paterson from Ringwood, New Jersey. Now things seemed to be happening for a reason. The move, the baby, the African-man and now the car, I was sure going to make good use of my lady having a car. I mean I had my own wheels, but compared to my wheelchair, a real car was a 747 jet to me.

The day had finally come and I still was not prepared for the move into the projects yet. The moving company had been working all day moving our things from the senior citizen building on Ellison Street to Building 11 Apartment 1A in the Alabama Projects. I had been listening to DMX's song, "Slippin'" all morning. I don't know what it was about that damn song but it motivated me in ways I never could explain.

My granny yelled my name from the living room. When my great-granny called my name I knew it was time. I turned the radio off and took a deep breath. I took one last look at my room and then the apartment. There were so many memories and good times that I was leaving behind. Yes, this was the end of the beginning. A tear rolled down my right cheek and dropped from my chin. I don't know why that feeling came over me but I couldn't fight it. Then my great-granny called me again. "Andre, let's go before you miss the bus."

Even though my great-granny and my granny and my

mom's had cars, my wheelchair couldn't fit in any of them. So I would have to drive my wheelchair to the bus stop to catch a ride to the new apartment. My mind was racing and I was lost in deep thought as I waited for the bus. I had heard so many horror stories about life in the projects that I was a nervous wreck. My stomach felt like there was a football game being played inside it. My palms were sweaty and my mouth was as dry as sandpaper. And then I remembered we had been so busy and preoccupied with the move I never even got the directions to Building 11. *Oh Lord*, I thought to myself as the bus passed block after block. What was going to do? I couldn't believe this had happened. I know my granny and them would be there waiting for me at the apartment.

When the bus finally approached my stop I was reluctant to get off but I couldn't ride the bus all damn day. I got off the bus on Market Street and started on my way up to the projects. I didn't know where the hell I was going. When I turned the corner I saw the huge building from a block away. My heart was pounding like it was going to jump out of my chest. When I was about a half a block from the projects entrance I noticed a large crowd in front of a liquor store. The name of the liquor store was Mr. Liquor. I didn't really know what was going on or why it was so many men and women out there. It seemed like they were all moving so fast. I saw the entrance to the projects. I was riding my wheelchair in the street because at that time all blocks weren't handicapped accessible. Now my heart was beating so fast it felt like I had just run a marathon. I was sweating like I had just jumped in a swimming pool. I was just about 10 feet from the corner when I noticed half the crowd staring in my direction. Oh, sweet Lord of mercy, why are they staring at me likes that? I didn't want to stop and I didn't want to keep moving forward but I had no other choice. All of a sudden in a blink of an eye there were 10 to 20 guys running toward me at top speed. I didn't have time to think or react it all happened so fast. I stopped my chair and closed my eyes and tightened up all the muscles that I could. I buried my head in my chest and took a long hard deep breath. I wondered which way I would fall when I hit the ground. I hope at least the casket could still be open at my funeral. My whole life flashed in front of me. And then all of a sudden I heard all this noise behind me. I opened my eyes and didn't see anything. I thought I heard the group saying, "Good and plenty, good and plenty." I turned my head to the rear and all the guys that had just run passed me were all around this car that had been slowly approaching. The men all had their arms extended out inside the vehicle. Then all the men walked back passed me like I was invisible. And one man trailed behind them counting money. And that's when it hit me like a ton of bricks. The men that ran past me were drug dealers, and the man in the car was a buyer. What

I thought I heard was not good and plenty but, "How many, how many…."

I felt like a chump and a sap sucker after the whole thing was over. I regretfully steered my wheelchair through the crowd on the sidewalk. I didn't have a clue in the world where Building 11 was. When I entered the complex the first building I saw was Number 5. A great feeling of relief came over me because I assumed if I just kept rolling I would definitely have to run into Building 11. There were people everywhere just chilling and hanging out. I looked out into the parking lot and noticed all kind of cars from new flashy cars to old models. Music blasted from car radio systems as the owners stood tall beside them. Fine women seemed to be in every direction I looked. I proceeded down farther and to my shock the next building I saw was Building 4. I paused and tried to catch my composure and not show my fear and how dubious I was. If I said I wasn't being stared at it would be more than a little white lie. I was used to being stared and laughed at like I was from prehistoric times. Then I could have sworn I heard someone say, "He looks like a scary mask." That's when I put my wheelchair in high gear and sped in the direction of the next building. Before I knew it I had almost reached the end and was parked in front of Building 2, when this older lady noticed I seemed lost. She had to be in her late forties. Her complexion was honey-brown and she stood 5'7" or 5'8". As she directed me toward Building 11, I noticed how white her teeth were and how nice her hair looked. To this day I have never forgotten that lady's face or her pretty smile and those pearly white teeth.

When I finally made it to my building, I was completely exhausted and mentally drained. Once inside the apartment I shook off the hysteria and gazed out the window for what seemed like hours. All the time I just kept saying over and over to myself, "What has my great-granny gotten me into?"

Chapter 17

I had been looking out of the window for what seemed like hours, when all of a sudden a thought crossed my mind. I had just made such an ass out of myself up in the front by the entrance. For some reason I didn't want my first day to end like that. My mind began to see-saw thoughts and ideas one after another. I couldn't let night fall being the little scary kid in the wheelchair. On the other hand, I was the little scary kid in the wheelchair. The scary kid that almost had a heart attack my first day at the projects (before I even entered the projects).

So I came up with this plan. I would go back outside and drive my wheelchair back out to the front. I would drive right back passed everyone with a gangster lean and the eye of the tiger. I had my motivation music playing, "24 Hours to Live" by Mase featuring the Lox, Black Rob and DMX. Anything by DMX would charge a person up! Just to hear that bark or growl could have a midget thinking he or she could take on a giant.

I heard my granny call my name as I bolted out of the door. I was too caught up and in deep thought to respond. I needed to show my new neighbors that I was cool too. As I flew passed buildings at my wheelchair's maximum speed I felt a surge of power. I nodded and waved to men and women, boys and girls. *Hey*, I thought to myself as I reached my destination, everybody's doing their own thing up here. If I said it once, I said it a million times. It was like the projects people were in their own world. And that was a world that I definitely wanted to and had to be a part of.

Once in the store I thought I heard someone call my name. It was someone calling my name. My granny had sent my little cousin to come look for me since I had left the house in such a hurry. When I saw him it killed the whole super cool vibe I was in. Why did granny send my little cousin out here to look for me? I quickly snapped back into superfly mode because my mission wasn't complete yet. I still had to make it back passed everyone with a look of confidence and cool. I had to make everyone think I was down, chill, cool and legit.

I bolted out the store on my way back passed the crowd. I was cruising now passing building after building. Some of the same people that had spoken to me coming spoke to me leaving. I felt accepted and strong as I let a little smile out. Maybe just maybe I could be welcomed with open arms. I didn't see anyone laughing or looking at me sideways. Coming back outside had been a great decision. My plan had worked like a charm. I leaned a little harder in my wheelchair just to add a little extra cool to my look. I had a real gangster lean going on. "Yes, yes, yes," I said over and over again under my breath. And that's when it happened, my whole world came crashing down on me. I thought to myself, this can't be happening. Not now, Lord, not now please! *My wheelchair broke down*!

I looked up in the sky and begged God to not let this happen. I tried over and over to see if it would work. It was dead and I was stranded. I sent my little cousin to get help. I slumped down in my chair and painfully waited for help as people, one after another passed and stared at me. Some would ask if I needed help and others would just walk by. When help finally arrived I was picked up and place in a car while my little cousin pushed the wheelchair home. My plan which started out great had turned into a classic and memorable blunder. My chair had broken down not far from my building but in plain sight of everyone. My first day in the projects had turned out to be one hell of a day! (And one I'll never forget for the rest of my life).

After that day I couldn't see myself ever going outside again. Before I knew it minutes turned into hours and hours turned into days, this had to be one of the most confusing and boring times of my life. I would just sit and gaze out the window all day, every day. I knew sooner or later I would have to break out of this mentally dead state of mind. Amy was sure she was ready to drive to Paterson from Ringwood. She had been practicing with the car her parents bought her for some time now. Even though there was so much going on in my life I really missed her. So we finally set up a date for her to come and get me from the projects.

When the day came I was more than ready. I had been cooped up in the house for what seemed like ages. It was about ten minutes before Amy was to arrive, so I decided to go outside and wait for her. I was in Building 11 but I was in apartment 1A which was on the first floor. Lord that was a blessing being on the first floor. On my way out the apartment the door next to mine opened and a lady greeted me with a huge friendly smile. That lady along with her three children would become my guardian angels. If I could write a book about them I would but it would take years before I could ever finish thanking them for all their love and support they showed and gave me during my time in the projects.

Amy arrived and picked me up and we burned rubber heading to the nearest hotel. It had been weeks since we had seen each other or touched each other in special ways. We laughed and joked around. The sex was overdue and intense. She insisted that we be careful because we didn't need another pregnancy. Amy parents had practically kidnapped my son from Amy and me. They had complete control and say over each and everything. In the back of my mind I knew it was for the best for my son. I wasn't in any form or fashion able to take care of a child. Damn, I was still living under my granny's roof.

Andre & My Nurse Alicia

It was getting very late and Amy had work and school the next day. I wished we could have stayed there for a year. I knew it was right back home to those four walls in the apartment. But one thing that Amy told me stuck in my mind. She told me that I had a way of touching people hearts without even trying. That the same magnetic attraction that made her come back to me after running away at the mall, was the same inner strength that would make people accept me in the projects. Everybody is special with special qualities because we are all God's children, and God doesn't make mistakes. She definitely had me thinking on the way to my building. Once inside my granny's apartment I told myself that starting tomorrow I would have a brand new attitude and mindset.

Chapter 18

The next day I woke up with a brand new attitude toward life and my new surroundings. I told myself if I was going to be the new little kid in the wheelchair with the scary mask face, then I was going to be the coolest kid in the wheelchair anybody had ever seen. I got dressed at about noon. I knew it was a good time to hit the streets. Just before I left out the door I put my fitted baseball cap on backwards and tilted it to the side. As I sped out the building at top speed I felt a rush inside my body that I had never felt before.

I blazed passed people one after another at maximum speed that my wheelchair allowed. Every time I passed someone I nodded with the coolest look I could muster up. Before I knew it I was at the store and shopping. After that I was on my way back to my building. The same way I soared coming was the same way I soared going. When I reached my building I was smiling from ear to ear. I thought to myself, mission accomplish without any problems.

And that's how things went day after day, month after month, and year after year. But one day as I was speeding passed some guys this one guy looked at me and said "Yo', man you one cool dude." The other guys that were with him all smiled and laughed with their approval and that was the day when I knew I was accepted into the project family. It felt good to be accepted, real good.

Amy was coming down to either pick me up or chill with me every day. Time was flying and at this time I found my one true love again rapping. If I wasn't listening to hip-hop, I would either be with Amy or my new best friend James.

James was a very important person in my life during those years. I always liked to say James was my eyes in back of my head. James was brown-skinned and wore braids in his hair. He was about 5'8" and stocky. He was the first person to teach me about all the opportunities for the handicap. All the paperwork and phone calls and things that needed to be done, he would help me with. We became very close friends. Just like there had been Wally and Angel, now God had sent me James.

Then one day out of nowhere my mother showed up. Her miracle relationship joyride had come to a crashing end. Yes, the best thing to ever happen to her was over just like that. Life was sure funny because for some reason I used to have this same dream every night that my mom would show up at granny's doorstep. And just like that it happened right before my eyes. Yes, those were some tough times following their breakup.

Around this time I was getting an urge to sell marijuana like a lot of the other guys were doing. I needed extra cash and I was eager to try. So I did. Everything was going quite well for me. James and I were hanging every day. Amy was still working and going to school and coming to see me all the time. She was beginning to like it at the projects. It was all new and I guessed the new but different environment was exciting to a Valley Girl from Ringwood, New Jersey.

About a month or two after my mom had moved in with us she showed up looking strange. And the last two months she would just pop up every now and then. She looked like she had lost a great amount of weight. And anybody who knew my mom knew she was known for having weight in all the right places. After that every time she showed up her appearance was either the same or worse. It didn't take a rocket scientist to know what was going on. It was official that my mother was smoking crack cocaine. She had fallen victim to the streets as it lured her to the almighty crack pipe.

You can do all the talking and begging and crying to a person on drugs but until they are ready to help themselves you're just wasting your time and breath. So once I knew my words were fallen on deaf ears I left it in God's hand. I trusted and loved my mother enough to know, she was a strong black woman and nothing, could keep her down not even the almighty crack pipe. Or so I thought.

Amy had begun to nag me all the time about letting her hangout with James's girlfriend. But I always had a bad feeling deep down inside about it. I would always tell her another time maybe. But she never stopped nagging me about it and it was beginning to eat away at me. So one time against my better judgment I let her hangout with James's girlfriend and some other girls. If I knew then, what I know now, I would have never let it happen. It was the beginning of the end for Amy and me. The projects were a whole new world and Amy wasn't ready for it. Within a month Amy was having sex with other guys including some of my new friends. They ran through her like a tornado crashing through a village.

At this time, things were really starting to happen around me fast. To top things off my mother OD'ed one day and she almost lost her life. I lost it when I heard the news. I sped into my house and grabbed a pistol someone had let me hold and rushed to the crack house at top speed. I don't know what I was going to do but I wanted to just hurt something. The pain I felt inside was too unbearable. I just wanted to hurt someone.

After the incident with my mom and my loss of Amy I knew it was time for me to leave. It had been seven long years in the projects and it was time for me to move on. James and I decided to become roommates. He put everything into motion and did all the paperwork. This would be my first apartment on my own. And whether I was ready or not it had to be done.

All and all, if I had to sum up my project experience up I would say it was great. I met a lot of good people and learned a lot about life. If there is anything I want people to know about my experience living in the projects is the projects are one big family. They had everything they needed right there: Laundromat, barbershop, beauty parlor, and liquor store and grocery store. Everything was right there within arm's reach. It took me seven years to understand but when I left the projects, I finally understood the name many had given it, and that name was the "The Lost World."

Chapter 19

When I left the projects James found us a nice two-bedroom apartment in Elmwood Park, New Jersey. It was beautiful like a breath of fresh air. I was on my own for the first time and it felt wonderful. James was working and handling the things I couldn't. We were more than just friends. We were a team like Batman and Robin. Amy was a distant memory. That's when the fun began. Chat rooms and girls was my daily pastime. Then the babies came one after another.

First there came Andre, born September 7, 2005, Jakayla, born February 15, 2009, Andrea, born February 23, 2011. And then my last one was Jaylin, born September 7, 2012. All and all, they gave me *five* children by *four* different mothers.

Before you start to judge me I want everyone to know that every woman that I ever loved, I thought would stay with me forever and become my wife. But it seemed that as soon as they gave birth to my child their disappearance would soon follow. I have been looking for answers to this for many countless years. It is a puzzle that haunts me each and every minute of the day.

Before I go any further I have to backtrack a bit. Getting out of the projects wasn't really that easy, especially without money and with my current situation of being disabled. James and I knew it was time to start calling everywhere and everybody. We knew there were agencies and foundations setup that would help someone in my predicament. I would often hear about support groups that were helping people like me all the time. Now knowing and getting them to help me were two different things. There was one thing I knew for sure, in this world it's always who you know.

One day I decided to call this number someone had given to me. I had been holding on to it for some time. After so many calls that went nowhere I was beginning to think moving out of the projects was just a thought or idea that would never turn into reality. You can say I was in desperation mode when I made the call. And that's when the Man upstairs who had come through for me so many times decided to deal me one more off the top. There was one more angel just waiting for me. I'm living proof that God might not come when you call Him, but He's always on time.

And this time my angel came in the form of a 5'10" medium framed white man with brown hair and glasses. He had a schoolteacher look. He had the friendliest smile and the coolest voice I had ever heard from a white man. His name was Mr. P. A. Chieffe, and he would unknowingly to himself or myself, become my social worker for the next 14 years. I cannot even touch the impact this man has had on my life in this paragraph, page or book. All I will say is that he has helped me in my adulthood more than anybody else in the world. Mr. Chieffe has gone above and beyond in his quest to help make my life and living situation the best it could be.

The strange thing about it is that when Mr. Chieffe set up the appointment to meet me it was to let me know he couldn't help me or take me on as another client. After I spoke to him on the phone we agreed to meet at the McDonald's on Market Street, about a block and a half away from the projects. As I entered the McDonald's and drove my wheelchair up to him I had one thing and one thing only on my mind. This was the man that was going to help me get out of the projects. As I got close enough to him a tear rolled down my eye as I extended my hand out to Mr. Chieffe. Mr. Chieffe would later tell me and others that it was a moment that he would never forget for the rest of his life. As we shook hands I stared at him with tears rolling down my face and said, "Hello. My name is Andre Williams. Can you please help me?"

Mr. Chieffe later said there was no way he could have turned me away. And from that day on he has been my social worker and the angel that single handily saved my life and propelled me into manhood.

Elmwood Park, New Jersey, was very quiet. It seemed like it a whole new and different world from what I was used too. I thought there was only one cop car in the whole town. And for some strange reason I thought it was crime-free.

Anyway, James and I were not only roommates but the best of friends. We motivated each other and since my mind seemed a lot more at ease I began to get back into my love for rapping. My time in the projects had only hardened my skills in rap. It's much easier to rap about things when you can see and live them on an everyday basis. Those seven years in the projects had filled my mind with hundreds and hundreds of rap songs.

I had made up in my mind a long time ago that I wouldn't let anything stop me from doing whatever I wanted to do. And I wanted and still want and will be the first rapper in a wheelchair. I know I have a hole in my throat. And I know it's hard to understand what I'm saying. I also know that I weigh as much as a 10 year old and people look at me as handicapped. And I know I have a lot to overcome to get where I want to be. So all I can say is step aside world here comes "Andre DreStar Williams" (DreStar is my rap name).

I had been in Elmwood Park, New Jersey, almost two years but it seemed like one. Most of the time I was either on the phone in the chat rooms or writing rap lyrics down for my next song on my album. I had met another young lady in the chat room and we had begun a relationship. We had been talking for some time, one thing just lead to another. Before I knew it conversations of moving in together had begun. Now

I would be lying if I said the thought of living with the opposite sex wasn't a major turn-on. I had lived with James for two years now and even though we had nothing but good times and fond memories, living with a women was a no brainier.

Her nickname was "Crow" and she was from Upstate New York. Unlike my last relationship, Crow was the complete opposite of Amy. Crow reminded me more of a Paterson chick. She was more how should I say it, 'hood. We were like Bonnie & Clyde. A better way to put it is by saying we were partners in crime. We did everything together and even a few things we shouldn't have.

So there was a situation that occurred and James ended up moving out and Crow became the first female I ever lived with. Things were fine for a while but just like the old saying goes, nothing good last forever. Well, there was one thing good or should I say great that came out of the relationship. Crow became the mother of my second child. All I can say was I had another healthy baby and I was very pleased with God. I don't regret anything I've done in my life. But here I was in another situation with a woman with my child and things were changing. Two months after the baby was born Crow was gone and so was my child. I had learned a valuable lesson in life. James and I had been like blood brothers and I chose a woman over him. He was family to me and we had a true friendship and love for one another. I

James and Me

Life
Humble L Ent.
H Dre ENT.

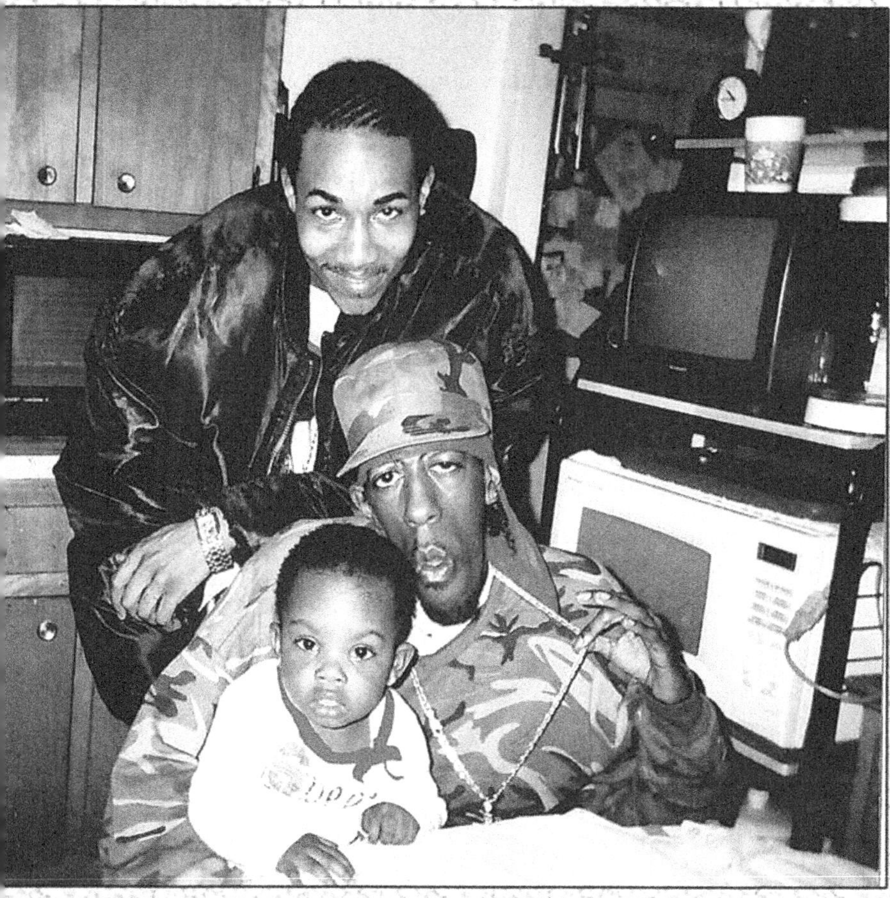

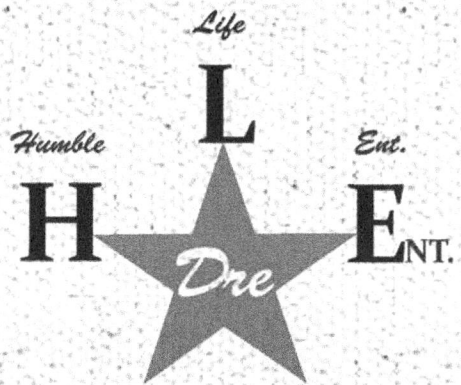

learned that girls, they come and go, but family is forever. I was growing up real fast, but still had a lot of growing up to do. Realizing this, the first thing I had to do was call James. This was a real big step in growing up, knowing and understanding that a real man can cry. Also not letting your ego get in the way when you're wrong and just be a man and apologize. And apologize I did with so much feeling and emotion that James knew it was coming from my heart. To make a long story short it wasn't long before James and I were roommates again in a brand new apartment.

Chapter 20

With James and me back together it was like we hadn't missed a beat. It was just like old times. James who also had skills in rapping suggested we really start trying to put our rap career in high gear. So whenever James was not at work we were working on raps. So my days consisted of chat rooms and rap music all day and sometimes all night. I really had a God-given gift in music (rap music).

The year was 2008, and I was 31 years old now. I sure would like to see the doctor who told my mother I wouldn't live past 12. I had defeated the odds that were given. Only God can determine the outcome of one's life, I'm living proof of that. For whatever reason God spared my life and extended it only He knows why. All I know is that I thank Him each and every day for giving me another day on His earth.

One night while I was on the chat line I met a young lady named Michelle from North Carolina. It didn't take long before we were in private chat. She told me she was white and didn't have a problem talking to an African-American male. I was excited like a winner of a sweepstake ticket. We talked and we talked for what seemed like hours. Before I knew it we were on the phone for hours and hours every day.

Michelle sent me a picture of her and she was beautiful. She had long blond curly hair like Shirley Temple. Her eyes were sky-blue and sexy. Her smile exposed pearly whites that screamed out, "No cavities in here." I was hypnotized by her beauty. I was sure when she got my picture it would soar through the air into the nearest trash can. But hey, I had come this far and there was no turning back. She received my picture and our phone relationship didn't skip a beat. After 1 month I was on cloud 7, after 3 months I was on cloud 9. And then we began to make plans for her visit to see me in New Jersey. If there was one thing I was good at it was making girls love me over the phone before we ever even met in person. I had done it with Amy, Crow, and now Michelle.

The date was set for Michelle to come visit. Amy had come from Ringwood; Crow had come from Upstate New York. But to meet someone from North Carolina, and expect them to come to New Jersey, to meet a guy in a wheelchair, I considered this a great feat. I'm not saying that they were vulnerable or I had the magic voice, but that the power of love was unbelievable.

The closer it got to the date for Michelle to come the more strange she began to act. I couldn't put my finger on it and it was starting to confuse me. In my mind I was starting to believe she was just getting cold feet or something. So I just tried to stay positive and assure my newfound love that everything was going to be all right. If I would say I hadn't grown attached to Michelle I would be telling a big fat white lie!

One night while we were on the phone Michelle said she mailed me a letter earlier in the day. We had been talking on the phone now for almost 3 months and it was about 10 days before she was to come to visit me. She told me she didn't want to talk to me anymore until I received the letter and read it from beginning to end. Before we got off the phone I thought to myself: *is this the way white women from North Carolina breakup with men?* I was at a loss for words and confused for the next couple of days. Every day I would rush to meet the mailman expecting the letter. I don't think I ever been that anxious for anything in my life. So four days after the phone call and six days before our scheduled visit the letter came. My hands were trembling as I ripped the letter open. My vision went from clear to blurry and back to clear as I began to read it.

Before I could even finish the first line a picture fell to the floor. I lean over in my chair and picked it up. It was the picture of an African-American woman. She had long silky hair and a light brown complexion. She had very sexy brown eyes with long eyelashes. The woman in the picture was a Jennifer Hudson look-a-like (before she lost the weight). I was confused and baffled. Why was Michelle sending me a picture of an African-American female?

It wasn't going to take long for me to find out because I was speed reading the letter now. When I was half-way through the letter I froze and dropped the letter to the ground. Michelle was Michelle but not the Michelle I had thought. My blond-haired blue-eyed dream was really a dream. It was all a lie because Michelle was 100% African-American. She had been misleading me for three months. I was devastated and couldn't believe she had lied to me like this and for so long. I was more concerned about if she would lie about her true self, then what other lies had she told me. In the letter she went on and on about not expecting this to ever go this far. She said that at first it was just a joke to her. Michelle said that she thought that since we met in a chat room it would be just a way to pretend to be white and have a little fun. She begged me to forgive her and accept her apology. All in all, I forgave her and made her promise not to ever lie to me again. Michelle said she loved me and would never ever lie to me again. So in 48 hours all was forgiven and no love was lost. But once again I learned a valuable lesson in life and this one I don't have to explain I'm sure you already know.

Chapter 21

Michelle called me to let me know she was about to board the Greyhound bus to New Jersey. I was overwhelmed with joy that she was actually coming. I made sure everything was perfect in the house. Also, I had set up a ride for her to be picked up at Newark Penn Station when the bus arrived. It seemed like that bus ride from North Carolina took 48 hours. But finally I heard the car pull up in front of the house, and when we made eye contact for the first time it was love or maybe lust at first sight.

When Michelle settled in, we talked for hours. The funny thing about it was that Crow was the complete opposite from Amy, and now Michelle was the complete opposite from Crow.

Michelle didn't smoke or drink. As a matter-of-fact she was somewhat religious in her own special way. She also made me aware that she was just here for a visit and would have to depart soon. She claimed New Jersey, was way too far from North Carolina, where she lived with her mother and brother. Well, needless to say, one day turned into two and two turned to three and the rest is history.

What I mean by that is Michelle would be in my life for the next three years and have my third child. Now she didn't really live with me for three years, but she would travel back in forth from North Carolina to New Jersey, twice a month or as much as possible.

Life was good.

James, who street pseudonym was "J-A" and I were still working on our rap career. Michelle and I were doing as good as a long-distance relationship could with all those miles in between us. When she was with me I was whole and complete, but when she was gone I felt something missing. I mean the phone conversations were good but there's nothing like having a warm body lying next to you. I guess that's just something I always loved was having my companion right there near me. Being by myself reminded me of the days when I yearned for companionship from the opposite sex.

Around this time my character was switching gears and I started thinking like a family man. So I decided if I was going to be a family man then I would have to work and support my family like a family man. In my heart I knew I could do it but in the back of my mind I knew there would be certain dilemmas. I knew that wherever I went to find a job they would have a problem with my dilatory movement. But ever since a kid I used to have one dream. My dream was to get a job as a ticket puncher or ticket ripper at the movie gate entrance. I always thought that would be a perfect job for me since I could stay in one spot and rip tickets all day.

At this time in my life the AMC Theater in Garden State Plaza mall in Paramus, New Jersey, was my favorite theater. I went there at least once to twice a month. I knew the layout and I'm sure all the employees had to be familiar with me. Hey, I'm the handsome guy in the wheelchair that's always here, I thought to myself. So anyway, it was just my luck that one day while I was there I noticed they were hiring for ticket puncher. My palms were sweating as I dial the number to inquire about the job. I was informed that I had to do the application online. Well, I did the application online and bingo they called me a couple of days after. I couldn't believe they called me so fast to come in for the interview. My mind was flustered with the thought of should I have told them about my situation. Hell, I figured this was America, the land of the free and the home of the brave. This is the United States where every disabled person gets a fighting chance and equal opportunity.

I knew about the "Americans with Disabilities Act" passed in 1990, which was supposed to open doors for opportunity. With all this being said I felt my disability couldn't and shouldn't factor in my being hired if I could perform the job duties. I also figured with 15 percent of the world's population being disabled there was at least one other disabled person employed there (or in the mall).

The day arrived for my interview and I was professionally dressed and looking very charming (if I

114

Andre

Life

Humble   L   Ent.

H ★ E NT.
Dre

should say so myself). I can't remember every piece of clothing I had on but I remembered my outfit consisted of: dress shirt with a nice tie and slacks. I had rehearsed the do's and don'ts that I was informed of like: keep eye contact, no gum, be on time, firm handshake and speak properly. I played the interview over and over in mind for days. When I boarded the bus for the mall I felt powerful and confident. The bus was my own personal limo and I knew the job was mine, all mine.

As I drove my wheelchair into the movie theater I began to get nervous. All my confidence was easing out of me like an airbag with a hole in it. Instantly I thought of my mother and great-grandfather. They always taught me that I was just as good, if not better, than the next person, and to never let anybody make you feel different or less-than a supreme being. With that in mind, I drove my chair right up to this lady (secretary) and asked for the manager. I told her, "I'm Andre Williams. I have an interview today." She gave me a weird look and frowned like I had just told her she had a booger on her nose. I tried to stay impassive but I began to sweat a little. She got up from her seat and walked over to this gentleman. I tried my best not to stare but they were directly to the right of me and maybe a few feet away. I noticed the gentleman look at me and back at her and began to laugh. And I don't mean a quick smirk or a giggle either. They were in full laugh mode.

Now, there is one thing I know, I know when I'm being laughed at. Trust me; I'd been laughed at enough times in my life to know.

Finally, the manager proceeded to walk over to me and introduced himself. I did likewise. He asked me what job I was applying for and I told him ticket puncher. He went on to tell me what sounded like the biggest bunch of horseshit I had ever heard. He told me that in order for me to be a ticket puncher I would have to first start off at the concession stand and work my way up. Then he let me know he would still give me the interview if I wanted it but it would just be a formality. Now, I don't know if he was being truthful or not but one thing I know for sure was that I never saw a person in a wheelchair working behind a concession stand.

To make a long story short I went on and had the interview and I did quite well. Once again I learned a valuable lesson in life. But there is one thing I'll say about this, *Welcome to the World of the Disabled*!

Chapter 22

While Michelle was visiting she received some bad news. Her brother had been killed in a car accident. She was devastated and mentally crushed. The news couldn't have come at a worst time. Our relationship was on the verge of being over and I was going through my own personal and financial problems. When she boarded that Greyhound bus on that cold rainy night, I never expected that it would be the end of our three year relationship. But here it was another woman leaving me within months of having my child.

After that I swore there would be no more chat room relationships for me. It was time for me to move on and in a huge way.

James had met a woman and started a family. He was always a hard worker anyway, so for him to settle down and become a family man was easy. I missed his company but I knew he was doing grown man things. So I decided to put sometime into me. I started playing with computers all the time. I wanted to learn as much as I could about them. Also, I started my own rap label: HUMBLE LIFE ENT. Meaning: *humble your life, entertain your soul.*

After six months I had become almost a wizard with my

computer. My rapping was taking off too. I had begun to write songs with no problem. Once I began writing the words just came together like a puzzle. It was like somebody was using me like a vehicle and steering me in the right direction. I hadn't talked in a chat room for six months, but I would be lying if I didn't say the temptation was killing me. I was a talker and a slick one at that but I had to stay focus on me.

Around the eighth month it seemed like the only thing that was missing from my life was those darn chat rooms. But every time I thought about the ladies I had met and the pain they brought I would shrug the thought off. After Michelle left I would have suicidal thoughts. And for some reason I couldn't get that damn movie theater manager laughing face out of my mind either. Of all the times I had been teased and laughed at that one always seemed to haunt me the most. Maybe because in my subconscious mind I really believed I had that job. After that I had never really thought about working again. Maybe that's why I took my rap career so seriously, because I could be my own boss with my own concepts.

It was New Year's Eve and it had been nine months since I last talked in a chat room. Being alone and the New Year approaching I finally gave in to the temptation and picked up my phone dialed the chat line number. When it started ringing I slammed the receiver down and just stared at the phone. It was as if I was a drug-addict fighting off relapsing. I shook my head and picked up the phone and dialed the number again. The operator voice went on and on with the rules and legal and illegal mumble jumble. Then I heard room 1 zero, room 2 zero, room 3 zero, I swear I started to hang-up when the voice said, "Room 4, 4." I figured ok its 4 people in this room let me see what kind of lying, cheating, crazy maniacs are in here. I said, "Hello, who in here?" And that's when I heard the sweetest and sexiest voice I ever heard. I froze and just listened to the four-way conversation. But every time I heard her voice it just sent chills up my spine. I continued to listen until there were just two voices left in the room. The conversation was slowing down so I spoke again, "Hello, who in here?" The sexy voice responded, "Jasmine. This is Jasmine." I almost fell out my chair as I said, "I'm Andre, Andre the handicap rapper." She giggled a little and that made me feel good.

We began to talk and we talked so long we ended up in private chat. "Well, Andre, the handicap rapper, what are you doing all alone on New Year's Eve? No one should be alone on New Year's Eve." She said. I began to explain why and how I was alone the day before New Year's.

Jasmine was from New York and out with her cousins. I don't know what made me say the next thing I said but it just came out. "Why don't you come keep me company, Miss Jasmine from Brooklyn? You only a hop skip and jump from me, and other than your cousins you're really alone too." She laughed and giggled again and said, "You crazy, I don't know you." I said, "Listen. My name is Andre Williams and I live in Hackensack. I'm not a serial killer or a rapist or anything like that. I'm in a wheelchair. I'm 5'9" and I never been in trouble in my life. Now there is one major thing that I must warn you about." I paused. "What is that Andre Williams?" Jasmine said. I said, "I'm extremely handsome and loveable." We both broke out in laughter. That was more than just laughter to me. Her laughter sounded like sweet music to my ears. It was her signature on the dotted line that she was coming.

We planned for Jasmine to catch the bus the same day, which would be New Year's Eve. I wanted us to be together when the ball dropped so we could bring the New Year in together. Jasmine and I had a connection and it felt great. If you ever met someone and it seemed like you knew each other before, then you know what I mean.

The day was moving quickly and time was flying. She had so much to do we could never lock down an actual time she would get on the bus. I began to worry but I still went out and bought some roses and a bottle of champagne. The sun was going down and nighttime was quickly approaching. I was beginning to think that Jasmine might back out. Her cousins were telling her she was crazy because she didn't really even know me. I was trying my best to convince her she would be all right. But in the background I could hear them yelling at her not to come.

I had to do something and I had to do it fast before my Jasmine changed her mind completely. I could hear it in her voice that she was undecided and not sure. So I blurted out, "Jasmine, I'll send a limo to pick you up." I know a limo driver with his own limousine. I could tell I had her undivided attention now. I could hear her telling her cousins I offered to send a limo. They were all whispering among each other. I quickly hung-up and called my friend and asked how much it would cost to pick someone up from Brooklyn and bring them to Hackensack, New Jersey. The charge was outrageous and he was supposed to be my friend. Now the only thing that separated Jasmine and me was a very expensive limo ride. Well, I won't talk about that limo charge anymore the fee has been hidden to protect the innocent fool who was blinded by a sexy voice and loneliness. In other words, it was too much damn money; the bus would have been cheaper, nineteen times cheaper if you do the math. So everything was set and the limo driver was on his way to pick up Jasmine. I guess after her cousins found out she was getting door-to-door service in a limo, it eased the tension a little but not much.

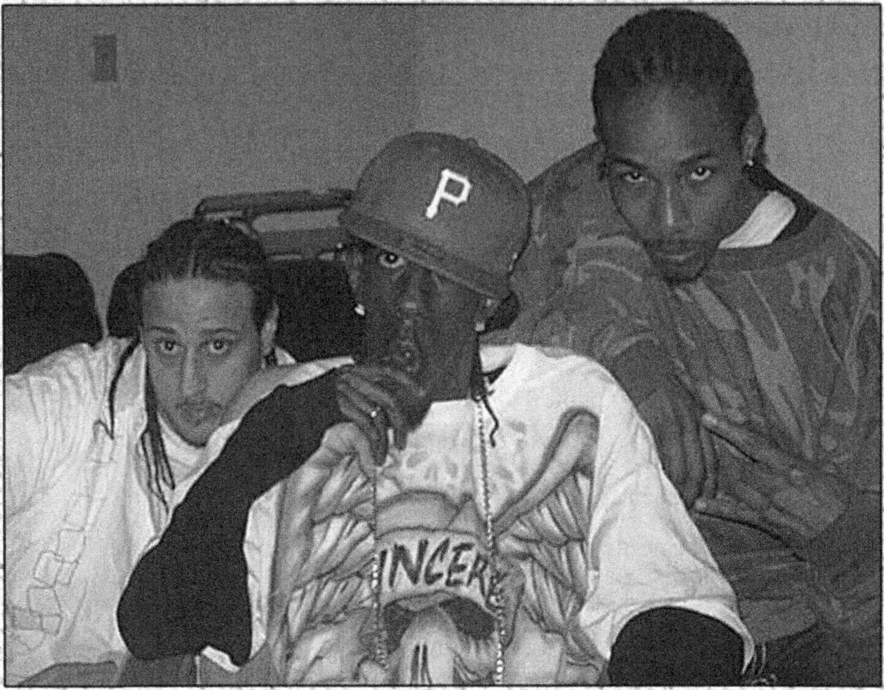

Wally, Me and James

Life
L
Humble H *Dre* ENT. *Ent.*

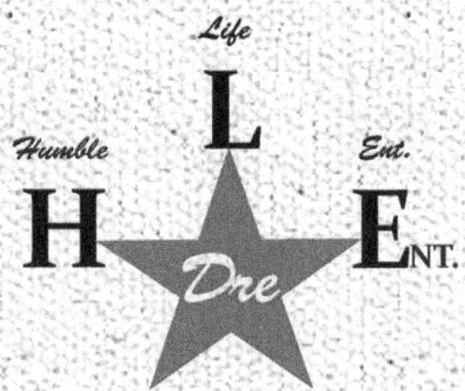

Chapter 23

While I waited for Jasmine to arrive I started getting everything ready. I wanted to make a good impression on her that she would never forget. I ordered Chinese food and set the table. I set the champagne bottle and two glasses on the kitchen table. I threw rose petals on the floor from my apartment door to the kitchen table. Then I got an even better idea. One that I knew would make Jasmine really feel welcomed and safe. I waited until they were about fifteen minutes away before I sprang into action. When I knew they were almost here I quickly exited my apartment and made my way to the elevator. When the elevator opened it was empty. I thanked God for that. I threw rose petals all over the elevator floor. Then I proceeded to throw more rose petals from the elevator to my apartment door.

When the limo pulled up my anxiety level was on one thousand. The limo driver rushed around the car to open her door. He was saying something about her cousins taking pictures of him and the license plates. I never really heard a word he said because my attention was focused on seeing Jasmine—the beautiful young lady with the golden voice.

When she made her exit from the limo she cracked a

smile, and that picture has forever been a fixture in my mind. She was light brown with a gorgeous complexion. She seemed to be a little shorter than me and medium built with shoulder-length hair. We entered the building and made our way to the elevators. It was now about 11:15 p.m., forty-five minutes before the ball was to drop. The elevator opened and when she saw the rose petals on the floor she gasped for air. We were in the elevator now on the way up to my floor. When the door opened I told her to follow the rose petals. She wanted me to go first and I wanted her to go first. We went back and forth with this for a minute or two until she finally gave in. She followed the rose petals to my apartment door and proceeded to walk inside.

When she opened the door she saw the rose petals leading her right to her chair at the kitchen table. Before I left the apartment I had turned off all the lights and lit candles giving it the candlelight dinner vibe. Jasmine sat down and began crying. I asked her did I do something wrong and was she ok? She replied, "I'm fine. It's just that no one has ever done anything like this for me before." I move closer and asked her could I touch her shoulders. All I know was that I wanted to comfort her during this moment.

After dinner we went into my bedroom to watch TV and talk. And talk, we did for the next three days. It was strange because just like Crow was different from Amy and Michelle was different from Crow, well, Jasmine was in a league all by herself because she was different from all three of them. Jasmine was beautiful inside and out. She was intelligent, honest, kind and someone I wanted to be around forever. I knew after those first three days we were soul mates, and she felt the same way about me.

On the third day as evening was approaching I told Jasmine I was going to take a shower. So after the shower I decided to play a joke on Jasmine. Well, most people don't know but being that I have muscular dystrophy, I'm able to bend and maneuver my legs in awkward positions. If I have on a loose T-shirt I can push my legs under the T-shirt with my kneecaps press against my chest and you would never even notice it as long as my arms were folded across my chest. So that's what I did and when I entered the bedroom. It looked just like I didn't have any legs. Jasmine was looking at me but she didn't say a word. I knew she probably was saying, "Oh, my God, he has fake legs too." I broke her trance and said, "Jasmine, can you go get my legs out of the bathroom? My legs fell off in the tub when I was taking a shower?" Jasmine never even said a word; she just jumped up and walked toward the bathroom. I waited a minute to give her time to get there and look around for my legs. Then I called her back into the bedroom and pulled my legs from under my shirt and said, "I got you, didn't I?" Jasmine began laughing uncontrollably and so did I.

Jasmine and I have been together almost five years now.

124

We have two beautiful children, Andrea and Jaylin. Jasmine's laughter is still music to my ears. Just like the first time I heard her laugh and giggle in that chat room. I knew then, just as I know now, that's one laugh I wanted to keep hearing for the rest of my life.

THE END

52780874R00080

Made in the USA
Middletown, DE
11 July 2019